W9-CBA-415

Authority

AUTHORITY

E. D. WATT

ST. MARTIN'S PRESS NEW YORK

Library of Congress Card Catalog Number: 82-42542

ISBN 0-312-06121-8

CONTENTS

INTRODUCTION

Recent writing on authority has been very extensive, as the attached bibliography shows. Yet over the same period it has become commonplace to hear it said that authority is in difficulties, in crisis, in decline. The institutions of family and school, of state and church are said all to have been affected by the decline of authority, and authoritative offices to be increasingly challenged by those subject to them, and increasingly burdensome to those who occupy them. But perhaps all this attention to authority is understandable enough. Men do not talk most about their health when their health is best, and if there has been increased attention to authority, this may be further evidence that those who believe that authority is in widespread decline are right.

Unlike health, however, authority does not seem self-evidently desirable. Authority is never egalitarian. An authority is always a superior of some kind, to be obeyed in some cases, in other cases to be followed, consulted, attended to, deferred to, or conformed to. It imposes constraints which are not always to the advantage of the person subject to it, and even when they are to his advantage, that will not always save him from finding them irksome. Authority in all its forms is associated with, and is a constant reminder of, some human limitation, weakness, or dependency. Even where the necessity for authority cannot plausibly be disputed, as in childhood, its progressive disappearance in due season is usually counted as a benefit. In some cases it will be possible without evident absurdity to hold that authority creates, and in other cases that it prolongs, the limitation, weakness or dependency to which it may appear to be an answer and a remedy. Authority, like strong drink, is readily associated with, and even identified with, its excesses and abuses: in the family, we are told, authority may delay, even prevent, the emergence of mature human beings; in government, that it facilitates, through submissiveness and apathy, the commission of far greater crimes than would otherwise be possible; in matters of

7

learning, that it stands in the way of people finding out things for themselves; and in matters of right and wrong, that any reliance on authority is incompatible with moral autonomy, with authentic moral conduct. We are reminded that bearers of authority are themselves no more than human, sharing in the human limitations which are said to explain and justify their authority. In a time when expressed sentiment, at least, is predominantly egalitarian, all relationships of authority, which are necessarily unequal relationships, are suspect. Even to consult a work of reference is to place oneself *in statu pupillari*. Anyone disposed to accept an authoritative claim is unlikely to remain long in doubt that the burden of argument lies with him, to justify his consulting, deferring to, or obeying an authority rather than relying on himself, finding out for himself, deciding for himself.

The aim of the present study is certainly not to reverse so formidable a tide; not to argue the claims of authority in general (if such a thing is conceivable), nor of any particular kind of authority; not even, except in passing, to evaluate arguments offered in support of the authority that goes with this or that activity or institution. Rather, it is to consider what authority means in some of the contexts where we find it, and how these various meanings are related. In this way, an approach not directly evaluative may move by more circuitous routes to consider in what matters, and in what measure, authority may in principle be dispensable, and whether we can conceive of human beings and human society without authority. If we can, then we may also imagine each kind of authority vacating the area of human conduct where it has hitherto been found. If we cannot, then it will still be possible to consider authority's limits and abuses, but it will be necessary to concede to authority, in an age inhospitable to it, at least the status of a necessary evil.

This study begins by considering what light may be thrown on the idea of authority by tracing it to its Latin origin. Some prevalent ways of confusing authority with the abuse of authority are then examined. The kind of compliance of one person with another without coercion or threats, without persuasion or bargaining, is something to which the word Authority is applied, and an attempt is made to see what can be said about such compliance simply as a fact, without reference to the reasons that people may have or the rules they may be following, when they comply with authority. It appears that authoritative compliance cannot long remain intelligible, either to participants or to observers, unless they understand the reasons or rules that go with it, and this in turn explains why the notion of an unlimited authority makes no sense: the reasons or rules which make each kind of authority intelligible by showing the point of it, also set bounds to it. The sense in which authority is ascribed to a learned person or a work or reference is then considered, and distinguished in principle from a right to be obeyed, while recognising that authority in those two distinct senses may occur together. What it might mean to ascribe moral authority to someone is explored, and then some of the ways in which the authority of religious institutions may be understood. Authority in the sense of a right to the obedience of subordinates, is then considered, together with attempts to ground such authority in the subordinates' consent, or in their needs, or in some other way. Finally, attention is given to some ideas about the nature of civil authority, and the distinction between it and other forms of authority.

Merely to add one more item to the list of recent publications on authority would be quite pointless. If, on the other hand, this body of writing illustrates some prevalent confusions about authority, then those confusions make it appropriate to examine afresh the concept of authority.

1 AUCTORITAS AND AUTHORITY

Words have their histories, which may throw light on their present meaning. The English word *authority,* and the corresponding words in other modern languages, take their origin from the Latin *auctoritas,* the meaning of which cannot be explained in a short space (*Thesaurus Linguae Latinae*, II, vi, 1231-2). It is related to the word *auctor,* and an *auctor,* according to Lewis and Short's Latin dictionary, is:

> He that brings about the existence of any object, or promotes the increase or prosperity of it, whether he first originates it, or by his efforts gives greater permanence or continuance to it.

A founder, an inspirer, an augmenter, or an ancestor can be called an *auctor,* just as in English a person can be called the *author,* not only of a book, but also of a policy or an enterprise. A parent, a patron, or a giver of advice can also be called an *auctor.* Clearly an *auctor* is in some sense a superior, not an equal, but his superiority is not necessarily in the sphere of command and obedience; more typically one defers to an *auctor* rather than obeying him, and some kinds of *auctor* (ancestors, for instance) cannot be obeyed at all, properly speaking.

As *auctoritas* is the activity or property of an *auctor* (Heinze, 1925, 349), the use of the word is correspondingly varied, and yet distinctive. *Auctoritas* was to be found in public and in private life. It was ascribed to founders, parents, tutors, patrons and givers of advice, to wise men and to ancestors. In a family, the earliest known progenitor was its *auctor,* and his successor in each generation inherited the founder's *auctoritas,* passing it on to his descendants, sharing in the founder's work as an *auctor* by augmenting and increasing what the original founder began. And like a family, Rome itself was thought to have an *auctor,* Romulus, whose act of foundation was the source of the civil *auctoritas* of

11

those who, in unbroken succession, were to share his work as *auctor* in time to come, by augmenting the Roman inheritance which in their turn they passed on to their successors.

Auctoritas in Roman republican government was not a right to rule; it was something quite distinct from the rights, *potestas* and *imperium,* to issue lawful commands which were legally enforceable. Each civil official had the *potestas* or the *imperium,* limited in time and in scope, that went with his office. Within these specified limits, his commands were legally binding. In addition, he possessed *auctoritas,* personal influence; and we have it on the *auctoritas* of Cicero that a Consul had *auctoritas* from the time of his nomination, but *potestas* only after he took up office (Mommsen, 1952, 1033-4). To the Senate, however, neither *potestas* nor *imperium* was ascribed, only *auctoritas.* It issued no commands with the force of law; indeed, it issued no commands at all, but only pronouncements in the form of advice — authoritative advice — to the civil officials in whose hands executive power lay. Its role was seen as deliberative and advisory, and its resolutions, however weighty, were styled *consulta.* The Senate's deliberations might make public policy, but it had no general executive power of its own, no means of giving legal effect to its own resolutions. To do that required the appropriate magistrate to adopt the Senate's advice and give it legal force by the exercise of his *imperium* or *potestas,* or legal ratification of the Senate's resolution by the *comitia tributa* or the *comitia centuriata.* This was usually done, but not always, and the law did not require it to be done. Likewise, an exercise of the legal powers of a magistrate might be endorsed, confirmed, ratified by the Senate, but was legally binding without that endorsement; the Senate had no legal power of veto or disallowance over the acts of consuls or praetors or tribunes. Mommsen speaks of the Senate's *auctoritas* as something more than advice (*Rathschlag*) and less than command (*Befehl*), as the kind of counsel which could not properly be shunned (Wirszubski, 1960, 113; Mommsen, 1952, 1033-4). Again, each magistrate had a set term of office, but the Senate was permanently in being. And, while the powers of a magistrate could be specified, and hence limited, the very idea of *auctoritas* was inhospitable to specification or limitation, and so hospitable to expansion. An official pronouncement can have great weight without having the force of law, and Wirszubski observes of the Senate's *auctoritas* that: 'Influence and the right to exert it are power, none the less real and legitimate for being undefined and not peremptory' (Wirszubski, 1960, 113). So *decree* is not an inappropriate translation for what Senatorial resolutions became, though they continued to be styled *consulta*.

The political importance of *auctoritas* was no less evident in imperial than in republican Rome, as the emperors brought together in their office *potestas* and *auctoritas*, the former by holding specific republican offices (or by holding and exercising the legal powers of those offices without holding the offices themselves), and the latter largely by drawing on the Senate's *auctoritas*. Augustus, emphasising the republican propriety of his constitutional innovations, claimed that he exceeded all men only in *auctoritas*, having no more legal power (*potestas*) than those who were his colleagues in the magistracies (specifically the consulship); and if the latter assertion was in some respects misleading, it would not be easy to dispute the former. By virtue of this *auctoritas*, Augustus was able to intervene, without provoking hostile reaction, in matters beyond the legal powers of the magistracies he held (Wirszubski, 1960, 114-16).

As the innovations of the principate lost their novelty, the emperor's legal power and his *auctoritas*, his command and his counsel, came to be more difficult to distinguish, since both issued from the same source: and though the legal status of the second kind of communication may still have been different from that of the first, the tone was not always less peremptory, nor the consequences of non-compliance less serious. The *lex de imperio Vespasiani* conferred on the emperor Vespasian legal powers without apparent limits, and responses to legal questions *ex auctoritate principis* (by the *auctoritas* of the emperor) came to be binding on judges at least by the reign of Hadrian (Wirszubski, 1960, 117). With the emperor issuing both counsel and command, deferring to weighty counsel was coming to be associated with, though not necessarily confused with, obeying lawful commands, and by the time, early in the sixth century, when the emperor Justinian proclaimed, in one of the great law-books issued during his reign, that he ruled *Deo auctore* (Constitution 'Deo auctore', in Justinian's *Digest*), his imperial predecessors had for five centuries been issuing both command and counsel, exercising both *potestas* and *auctoritas*. But there continued to be a Senate, discharging its remaining functions largely by the diminished weight of its *auctoritas,* though by the beginning of the third century its decrees had the force of law, without further ratification.

Roman civil *auctoritas* was traced to the foundation of the city, a unique event which could never be repeated; there was only one Rome, and it could be founded only once. Greek cities could multiply, setting up new foundations all over the Mediterranean, and in this way the Greek world spread. Rome could spread only by extending the original and unique foundation, incorporating other cities as subject municipalities. *Auctoritas* had to do with preserving as well as with founding, and, as the foundation was uniquely important, the preservation of what had been established was correspondingly important. It has been observed that there is no word in Greek to translate *auctoritas* (Mommsen, 1952, 954, n.4; Heinze, 1925, 363), and perhaps rather more debatably, that even the idea of weighty counsel, 'more than advice and less than command', is not to be found there either, at least in Greek political practice, which knew command and coercion of subordinates, and persuasion of equals, but not *auctoritas* (Arendt, in *Nomos* I, 1958, 84; Bambrough, in Laslett, 1956, 98-115). Both Bambrough and Arendt emphasise the novelty of Plato's and Aristotle's attempts to introduce such a notion into Greek political thought, drawing their examples from alien spheres: in Aristotle's case from the role of parents in the household, and in Plato's case from the arts and sciences, spheres of expertise, in which those who know make authoritative pronouncements. Indeed, it is more a right to make pronouncements than a right to command, which can be sustained by Plato's argument from the analogy of the physician's or the helmsman's art (*Republic,* VI, 488a), and some of the shortcomings in Plato's argument, though perhaps not all of them, spring from his attempt to extend its force from pronouncing to commanding, from *auctoritas* to *potestas.*

The scope of *auctoritas* in Rome was much wider than that of government. Parents had it in relation to their children, tutors to their pupils, patrons to their clients, the old and the wise in relation to everyone else, and the dead in relation to the living. Knowledge (*scientia*), and even the magic art, are said to have *auctoritas*. To augurs, to priests, and to the gods themselves *auctoritas* is attributed, and indeed the role of the Roman gods in relation to mortals was thought of more as approving, confirming and warning, than as commanding and forbidding — *auctoritas* rather than *potestas* (*Thesaurus Linguae Latinae,* II, vi, 1229, 1230, 1233). And, though the writers of Christian antiquity express a much clearer notion of divine command, they follow their pagan predecessors in speaking of the *auctoritas* of God, as well as the *auctoritas* of priests and bishops (*Thesaurus Linguae Latinae,* II, vi, 1230, 1231). Pope Gelasius I, late in the fifth century, contrasted the *auctoritas* of the papal office with the emperor's *regia potestas* (Migne, *Patrologiae Latinae,* 56, 634). In the Latin bible, however, *auctoritas* is never ascribed to God, but always *potestas*, and it is with *potestas* that Christ endows the apostles (*Matthew* 7:29, 28:18; *Luke* 9:1-2). Tertullian, Jerome, Augustine and others speak of the *auctoritas* of scripture and of its authors (*Thesaurus Linguae Latinae,* II, vi, 1224, 1225), and Augustine speaks of the *auctoritas* of the Church as a necessary condition for accepting that of scripture (Augustine, *Epistola Manichaei,* 5). The Church, like the Roman government, looked to its foundation and its founders as the source of the *auctoritas* which it had received from its divine *auctor,* and which present members would pass on to successors.

Some of these vessels of *auctoritas,* such as ancestors or predecessors, were incapable of issuing commands, so that acceptance of their *auctoritas* could only mean deferring to their counsel or example, and could not mean obeying their commands. Other vessels of *auctoritas,* such as the clergy or the emperor, were thought also to have *potestas,* a right to issue commands that ought to be obeyed, as well as counsel that ought to be respected.

The latter association holds when we turn from Latin to English. Like the emperors and the later Senate, and unlike its Latin original, the English word *authority* lives not solely in the sphere of counsel, but also in that of command, *potestas* as well as *auctoritas.* The *Oxford English Dictionary's* first entry on *authority* refers to command and obedience, and the fourteenth century use of the word first cited is in reference to a decree. Other fourteenth-century citations in the *OED* refer to counsel, testimony and example, showing that the English word had not lost these meanings carried by the Latin *auctoritas.* The King James bible, itself called *authorised,* uses the word extensively: Christ is said to have spoken as one having authority (*Matthew* 7:29), and to have been challenged to show what authority he had (*Mark* 11:28-9); but also to have *power* over all flesh, and *power* upon earth to forgive sins (*John* 17:1-2, and *Luke* 5:24), where in all these cases alike the Latin bible used *potestas,* not *auctoritas.* And when Shakespeare, at about the same time, uses the word *authority,* it is with a range of meanings (authority-on, authority-over, authority-with) not recognisably different from our own, e.g.:

Small have continual plodders ever won
Save base authority from others' books (*Love's Labour's Lost,* I, i)

. . . but man, proud man
Drest in a little brief authority (*Measure for Measure,* II, ii)

and

You have that in your countenance which I would fain call master.
What's that?
Authority (*King Lear,* I, iv)

Oddly enough, the word authority is not usually applied in recent times to the role of constitutional monarchs. When Bagehot, a century ago, listed the British monarch's constitutional rights as 'the right to be consulted, the right to encourage, the right to warn' (Bagehot, 1966, 111), he was ascribing to the monarch something more restricted in scope, a pale reflection of, but similar in nature to, the *auctoritas* of the Roman senate, but he did not use the related English word authority. Indeed, in becoming constitutional monarchs, kings and queens are sometimes said to have 'lost authority', when in fact it is rather their *potestas* that has been eroded (though by no means completely destroyed), while their *auctoritas*, 'more than advice and less than command', has in some cases suffered little or no loss.

Authority, then, is a word with a range of meanings considerably broader than its Latin original, extending to cover *potestas* as well as *auctoritas*. This seems to have been the case for as long as the English word has been used. So it is clear at the outset that to consider authority is to consider a group of ideas and not a single idea: to distinguish the more important of these ideas from one another, and to show, where it can be shown, how they are related.

IDENTIFYING AUTHORITY WITH ITS ABUSE: AUTHORITARIANISM, AUTHORITARIAN PERSONALITIES AND SHOCKING EXPERIMENTS

Authority, in some ways of talking about it, must be marked by the appropriate kind of reason or justification, so that whatever lacks that reason or justification cannot be authoritative. Accordingly, usurped authority is not a variety of authority, any more than an imitation pearl is a variety of pearl; an official who is exceeding his authority is no longer acting authoritatively; an unreliable work of reference is not authoritative; and a charlatan, lacking the learning that he is mistakenly believed to have, cannot be called an authority on his subject.

The related word *authoritarian,* on the other hand, carries a derogatory tone. A scholar may be commended as authoritative, but if he is said to be authoritarian he is not being commended. In the same way, the word is applied to families where the parents are said to be overbearing, and to governments which are said to be unreasonably restrictive and coercive, that is, to situations where the appropriate kind of justification is not present but absent, or at least inadequate in some way. In the typical usage found in one book on 'authoritarian politics', authoritarianism is associated with 'repression', 'internal passports and informer systems', and 'a full-scale garrison-police state', and in one place the expression 'authoritarian methods' seems to be a synonym for 'unfair electoral practices' (Huntington and Moore, 1970, 383). Jouvenel writes of this usage as a 'corruption of the word . . . of quite recent date' (Jouvenel, 1957, 30), but the word itself seems to be of quite recent date, the *OED*'s first English entry being as late as 1879, and there does not seem to be an earlier usage, of which the later usage is a corruption. Applied to government, the most obvious shortcoming of the word *authoritarian* is that it blurs the distinction between governments that run extermination camps and governments that merely run a press censorship office. Applied to individual persons, it may in nearly every case be usefully replaced by some less ambiguous word, according to the meaning intended: severe, domineering, intolerant, harsh, unjust, merciless, or whatever.

The application of the word to individual persons was given wider currency in the 1950s by the work of Theodor Adorno and his associates, published under the title *The Authoritarian Personality:*

> the major theme of the work is a relatively new concept — the rise of an 'anthropological' species we call the authoritarian type of man (Adorno, 1950, ix)

Contrasting in all things with his opposite number, called the democratic type of man, the 'authoritarian' is a bully, but is easily bullied himself; he is subservient as well as domineering. He is marked by conformity, rigidity, dependence, intolerance and cruelty; by superstition, suspicion, power orientation and unimaginativeness; by oversimplified dichotomising, intolerance of ambiguity and an undue preference for symmetry, familiarity, definiteness and regularity. Because he shows 'extreme susceptibility to fascist propaganda', the authoritarian man is said to be 'potentially fascistic', and is in some places called simply *fascist*. His propensities are assessed (the authors would say *measured*) by reference to something called the *F*— (for Fascism) *Scale*.

The shortcomings of this regrettably celebrated work have not gone unperceived (Christie and Jahoda, 1954), but most of them need not concern us here. By their oversimplified dichotomising, intolerance of ambiguity, and undue preference for symmetry, the authors have left room only for the one variety of 'authoritarians' they were looking for, the xenophobes (particularly the anti-Semites), and all but obscured others, notably communists. Of more interest here is the authors' association of this 'species of man' with authority. Such persons are represented to us as being interested in domination and submission whether rightful or not. They are not, we are told, subservient only to their rightful superiors, to those who have a right to their obedience, but to anyone who is stronger than they are, nor do they domineer over subordinates only within the limits of any authority they may have. Indeed, it is to situations of unjustified command and obedience that our attention is directed under the description of authoritarianism: to parents or governments considered by the authors to be unjustifiably restrictive, to officials who go outside their commission, and so on. Authoritarianism, then, has to do not with authority, but with the misuse of authority; not with authority appropriately justified, but with authority exceeded or abused.

The Authoritarian Personality may also be taken as an instance of the kind of attempt, frequently made, to associate a 'species of man' with a corresponding species of government. We are told that Authoritarian Personalities, because of their 'extreme susceptibility to fascist propaganda' (Adorno, 1950, 1), are likely to catch any fascist infections that are going around, so that where such people are numerous, fascists will have the potential supporters they need to build up fascist movements and to establish and carry on fascist governments. Anything that can be done, by appropriate child rearing practices or by subsequent exhortation, to reduce the incidence of Authoritarian Personalities and to produce more Democratic Men will do something to deprive fascists of such potential supporters — so the argument seems to run.

What this account would seem to neglect is that any large movement or organisation, and any government, must take people as it finds them, in all their variety. Rebellions are not conducted exclusively by men of highly rebellious temperament, or opposed exclusively by men personally less rebellious. Organisations must function as best they can with staffs which include men remote from the model of the Organisation Man (Whyte, 1957). And we have been given no reason to believe that Hitler's government was conducted in a country where the variety of personalities differed from what prevailed in Germany previously or subsequently. It seems beyond dispute that there can be profound changes in the climate of opinion and in the government of a country which cannot be attributed to correspondingly great changes in the personalities of its citizens, just as the foreign policy of a government may remain stable while foreign ministers with widely divergent personalities come and go.

But it is not out of place to associate government with individual obedience and the propensity to obey, since every government depends in large measure upon voluntary obedience: Hume reminds us that even a ruler who drives his people like beasts must do so by means of closer associates whom he leads like free men, by opinion (Hume, 1953, 24). Great achievements and great crimes of governments would be impossible if they could find no subjects who would obey orders.

It is not surprising, then, that Stanley Milgram permits himself some political generalisations well beyond the scope of the experiments which he writes up in *Obedience to Authority* (Milgram, 1974). In these experiments, voluntary participants were told that they were taking part in an investigation to ascertain the effect of pain on rates of learning, and that their role was to control a switch administering graduated electric shocks to other subjects when they could not recall memorised material correctly. These shocks, they were told, were harmless, but painful, and the experiment required that they be continued and intensified despite the apparent distress of the person who was said to be receiving the shocks. Most of the participants continued for a long time to operate the switches as the experimenter instructed them to do, ignoring the pleas of their victims. Their doing so was regarded by Milgram, quite rightly, as very disquieting.

In fact there were no electric shocks, and the distress of the victims was entirely feigned. But those working the switches seem to have believed that it was real, and Milgram marvels at their being prepared to continue participating in the 'experiment' as long as they did, when they had learned from childhood it is a fundamental breach of moral conduct to hurt another person against his will (Milgram, 1974, 41). If this is indeed what they had learned, their moral education would seem to have been unacceptably narrow, in taking no account of the justifiable infliction of pain (in setting a broken bone, for instance). But if such infliction of pain is justifiable, it is for weighty reasons; the reason in this case, experimental curiosity, is comparatively trivial, if real pain is to be inflicted, as Milgram's subjects were told it was. Moreover, his subjects might well reply *ad hominem,* that Milgram had no doubt learned from childhood that it is a fundamental breach of moral conduct to tell lies, or to instruct subordinates to perform cruel acts, and yet he had told lies to them about the nature of the experiment in which they were participating, and issued the very instructions which he later condemned them for obeying. In this respect at least, it seems reasonable to suggest that Milgram had exceeded his own authority as an experimental director.

He might plead in his defence that the experiment could not have been conducted unless he had told those lies and given those instructions, and that the valuable end justified the indispensable means. But his subjects could defend themselves in the same way: they also believed, for he had told them, that they were participating in an important experiment, to which the pain that they were inflicting was indispensable, and that the valuable end justified the indispensable means.

Milgram would not accept their defence, for he holds that good ends (which is what he seems to mean by 'ends . . . consistent with generally held cultural values' — Milgram, 1974, 176) do not justify the use of such means as the intentional infliction of pain against the expressed wishes of the victim. His contention would seem to be that means which are wrong in themselves cannot justifiably be used, even to attain a valuable end; but he does not explicitly say so, and if this is his contention, he has contravened it himself in the course of his own experiment. Moreover, he seems to consider that the root of his subjects' moral shortcomings is their propensity to obey authority — he cites Laski's essay 'The Dangers of Obedience' — and that they need to be more ready to disobey authority. Milgram, like Adorno and his associates, identifies authority with its abuses. This is misleading. Where authority means a right to be obeyed, such a right cannot be thought of except in association with the limits proper to it. If psychological experiments are to be conducted, directions must be issued to subjects, and someone must have the right, within the limits appropriate to the activity, to issue them. But to speak of a right to command wrongdoing can make no sense. When the subjects obeyed, it was not authority that they were obeying if the man in charge of the experiment commanded wrongdoing, for then *ipso facto* he had exceeded his authority. And those who disobeyed were not disobeying authority either. The 'disappearance of a sense of [personal] responsibility' that Milgram observes in his subjects would hardly be possible without some measure of confusion in their minds about the rightful scope of an experimenter's authority. If '. . . the subject acts within the context of a learning experiment and sees the experimenter's commands as meaningfully coordinated to his role' (Milgram, 1974, 8, 141), then the subject's notion of an experimenter's role may be far-reaching indeed. It is to such confusions that Milgram should have directed his readers' attention. To deplore authority, to seek to minimise it, to commend disobedience, is undiscriminating and confusing. Disobedience is not always praiseworthy, any more than obedience is, and it is hardly going too far to say that what Milgram proposes in place of undiscriminating obedience is undiscriminating disobedience. Many of Milgram's experimental subjects had evidently given very little attention to what may reasonably be included within an experimenter's role, or to what kind of command must clearly lie outside it.

The same may be said of Milgram's observations on military authority and obedience. Here, too, he confuses authority with the abuse of authority. He believes that soldiers exhibit, in a more serious form, the same moral shortcomings as his experimental subjects:

> . . . in wartime a soldier does not ask whether it is good or bad to bomb a hamlet; he does not experience shame or guilt in the destruction of a village; rather he feels pride or shame depending on how well he has performed the mission assigned to him. (Milgram, 1974, 8)

Here Milgram goes beyond his evidence, and beyond what is probable. Some of his own experimental subjects were reluctant to obey, and a few refused to obey, the instructions he gave them, and it is likely that some soldiers at least respond similarly when ordered, for instance, to kill prisoners. Milgram's complaint against his country's soldiers in Indo-China is against specified kinds of action that they performed: they

> . . . routinely burned villages . . . defoliated vast areas of the land, forced the evacuation of the sick and the aged for purposes of military expediency, and massacred outright hundreds of unarmed civilians. (Milgram, 1974, 180)

This is an odd list: the last item can be nothing less than an allegation of mass murder, compared with which the previous items on the list are morally trivial.

What they have in common is that Milgram believes that none of them may rightly be done in the conduct of war by soldiers acting under orders. We would do better, then, to approach the difficulty directly, not by objecting in general to military authority and obedience, but by considering what kinds of harm a government at war may be justified in inflicting on its enemies, and on the other hand, what kinds of act may be beyond the competence of military superiors to command, or of their subordinates to obey without fault. Unjustified commands are not instances of military authority, but abuses of it. A soldier obeying such commands cannot justify his action by saying that he is only obeying authority. What he is obeying, perhaps from fear, habit or a mistaken sense of duty, is the unjustified command of an individual who is exceeding his authority.

When authority is frequently and gravely abused, critics may lose interest in the distinction between authority and the abuse of it. Nonetheless, the distinction is well worth preserving. It is pointlessly confusing to use the same word for authority and for the exceeding or abusing of authority, to follow a usage in which

> . . . if violence fulfills the same function as authority, namely makes people obey, then violence is authority . . . authority is whatever makes people obey. (Arendt, 1956, 416)

And if people acting under orders are often prepared to administer electric shocks, and other harms very much more serious, the distinction between authority and its abuse needs to be more clearly drawn; to run them both together is undiscriminating, and darkens counsel.

3 DE FACTO AUTHORITY

When we observe one person conforming, in act or belief, in response to the suggestion, the example or the command of another, we may have reason to believe that he has been drugged or coerced, or, on the other hand, that he has been persuaded, or bargained with. In none of these cases would we call the relationship between them one of authority. In so far as we attempt to persuade or to bargain, we approach one another as equals, whereas authoritative relationships exist between unequals: between master and novice, superior official and subordinate, leader and follower. Again, we distinguish between conformity which is the outcome of coercion, and conformity which is not, and examples of authoritative conformity are commonly chosen from the second group: such cases as when advice is sought, or mannerisms are aped, or when a person takes charge of the evacuation of a burning building, and is obeyed. The point of choosing these examples is that the leader or superior has no means of coercing his followers or subordinates, so that if they consult or conform, their conduct must be understood in some other way.

So we find expressions such as *the phenomenon of authority, positive authority, informal authority, de facto authority* and *authority-with* (Peters, in Quinton, 1967) being used to distinguish that area of conformity which cannot be ascribed to coercion on the one hand, or to persuasion or bargaining on the other. This sense of authority is sometimes said to be strictly descriptive, having to do with the *fact* of compliance, having nothing to do with any right to command or obligation to obey. The evidence for authority, so understood, is the same fact of compliance, without coercion or persuasion or bargaining. In this sense, authority is not said to be bestowed, delegated, exceeded, abused, or revoked; rather it is said to be increased, gained, used, reduced, or lost. This usage corresponds with Kelsen's notion of the efficacy of law, which he distinguishes from the validity of law (Kelsen, 1945, 29-44).

A person *having authority with* another need not have any office or official standing. We find no difficulty in saying that an official has 'lost authority with' his subordinates while remaining *in authority over* them, that is, while retaining a right to their compliance which, in practice, he cannot get. And if, in practice, he cannot get compliance, that is sufficient evidence that he has lost positive or *de facto* authority. Likewise, we do not speak, in this context, of a person exceeding his authority, going beyond its rightful scope or limits, or acting *ultra vires,* for such authority has no rightful limits, no limits at all except the limits of the holder's capacity to secure compliance, and so Jouvenel can call authority, in this sense, a faculty, 'the faculty of inducing consent', Easton can call it a property, Friedrich a capacity, and Blau an ability of the holder (Jouvenel, 1957, 29-32; *Nomos I,* 1958).

Again, it is hard to see that there can be such a thing as spurious authority, in this sense of authority. Friedrich speaks of false or faked authority (*Nomos I,* 1958, 37), and indeed a charlatan or a lunatic may be obeyed or consulted or deferred to, because of false claims which his followers accept as true. Nevertheless, though his claims are false, it would seem that his authority must be called genuine, provided only that it is effective. A brigand, a rabble-rouser, a troublesome but influential schoolboy must be said to have authority with those whose actions or beliefs he influences, however false the claims he makes in support of his authority, if this use of the word is to be entirely non-evaluative, descriptive, 'positive'.

Of course, the one person may sometimes obtain compliance by the weight of his authority, at other times by persuasion, by bargaining, or by coercion. Likewise, he may be in a bargaining relationship with one group of people, a coercive relationship with another group, and an authoritative relationship with a third group. Moreover, in practice several means of obtaining compliance may be found together and may supplement one another. Bargaining or persuasion may sometimes be more effectively carried on with the aid of authority, even though to the extent to which he attempts to persuade or to bargain, a person is acting like an equal, and not like a superior. In the same way, success in bargaining, in persuasion, or in coercion may make it less necessary to use again these means of obtaining compliance, and more practicable to rely on something approaching pure *de facto* authority. And if the same person may sometimes coerce, sometimes persuade or bargain, and sometimes lead effectively without these means, that does not prevent us from distinguishing one from another. The ideas are no less clear in theory for their manifestations commonly being found mixed together in practice.

De facto authority, then, always implies a capacity to influence other people. Influence, of course, is a looser and far less discriminating term than authority: a skilful user of force or threat, or an able negotiator, may be also said to exercise influence, but could not properly be said to be exercising authority. Sometimes, however, the words are used almost interchangeably. Easton, in writing of the word authority, applies it to situations where one person complies with another's wishes because he likes him, or is afraid of him, or because he has been threatened by him, or to further his own material interests (*Nomos I*, 1958, 181-3). It seems quite misleading to use the word authority so loosely, nor does common usage support such an extension. Employment can be found both for a more specific word like *authority,* and for a more general word like *influence,* and nothing is gained by using them interchangeably.

As with influence, so with power: *de facto* authority may be said to imply power over those subject to it (Weldon, 1953, 51), since their behaviour is altered. A person who can be called powerless, cannot be said to 'have authority with' anyone, whatever office he may hold. If the possession of power is denied, as it sometimes is, to those who have *de facto* authority, this denial usually rests on the voluntary nature of authority-following, whereas 'in exercising power, a man secures compliance by force, threats or bribes . . .' (Benn and Peters, 1959, 297). But it seems odd to say that a man has no power over those who ask his advice or obey his commands or follow his suggestions voluntarily; it is preferable to use the word *power* broadly enough to cover all these situations, voluntary and involuntary alike, reserving the word authority, in the present *de facto* sense, for situations of unforced, un-threatened and un-persuaded compliance.

But not all instances of compliance are of the same kind, and the sense in which compliance with authority is voluntary will vary from situation to situation. The clearest cases are those involving command and obedience: a command cannot be obeyed involuntarily, any more than a command can be given involuntarily. But there are cases of compliance with authority which do not involve obedience to commands. B may comply, in act or opinion, with suggestions made by A; or B may take A as his authority, following A's example in matters of speech, dress, or mannerism, although A has never spoken a word to B, even of suggestion. In this way, A can have authority with people he has never met, never intentionally communicated with. And those who follow his authority do so voluntarily, but only in the weak sense that they are not coerced or persuaded or bargained with; they may scarcely be conscious that they are following, and even habitually following, his example, particularly if the adjustments which they make to their own behaviour are minor ones. But to obey a command is always voluntary in a stronger sense which involves *recognising* the communication as a command, and complying with it intentionally. Unless these conditions are met, we may speak of a suggestion being followed, or of merely accidental or inadvertent compliance; we do not speak of a command being obeyed.

De facto authority is a notion that involves looking at behaviour primarily from the perspective of the observer rather than that of the people whom he believes to be following authority. The observer may not know, and for his purposes may not need to know, how those subject to an authority understand their role in following it. And the more insistent an observer is that he is simply describing the fact of compliance with authority, the more strictly he will need to avoid the use in the same context of such ambiguous words as *legitimate*, or *approved* (de Grazia, 1959, 321-2; Catlin, *Nomos I*, 1958). If such a word means no more than *accepted*, then it is hard to see what it adds to this meaning of the word authority, which, as we have seen, has the notion of acceptance built into it; if, on the other hand, it means *justified*, then the enterprise of considering authority *de facto*, the fact of voluntary compliance, in a non-evaluative way, is at an end; and if the fact of voluntary compliance is held to *constitute* the justification of an authority, that standpoint will need separate argument in support of it (see Chapter 8).

The notion of *de facto* authority, then, allows us to ask only a narrow range of questions about authority. It carries the limitations, as well as the advantages, of human behaviour observed from the outside, as we might observe the leader-following behaviour of sheep. Such a perspective involves the danger of forgetting that authority, even authority *de facto,* has to do with human conduct. Our understanding of human beings complying with authority involves the possibility of their ceasing to do so. Material objects, animals and human beings may all be said to follow, to conform, or to obey, but not in the same sense. Projectiles are said to obey the laws of motion; but it would make no sense to speak of their *disobeying* the laws of motion, and animals, which are sometimes said to disobey as well as to obey, can hardly be said to have a *reason* for their disobedience, or to *pretend* to obey, as human beings can. The difference lies in the capacity of human beings to know what it is to act for some reason, to follow a rule or to obey a command. Even to consider in general what conditions are favourable to the loss or gain of *de facto* authority, is to see people more as responding passively and predictably to these conditions than as conducting themselves in a particular way for certain reasons or according to certain rules. The observer is not observing the behaviour of sheep, but must conduct himself as though he were, eschewing all evaluation, never speaking of authority as legitimate or spurious, exceeded or abused, and attending solely to the fact of voluntary conformity. It is not an easy standpoint to sustain for long.

REASONINGS, REASONS AND RULES

If a person is not aware that he is complying with authority, it will be out of place to ask him for the reasons why he is doing so. If, on the other hand, he complies intentionally, he will always be able, and may be willing, to communicate to an observer some notion of his reasons for complying. The observer, following Weber, may then classify the authority relationship as charismatic, traditional, or rational-legal; in doing so, it would appear that what he is attending to is the subjects' own understanding of their compliance with authority. Or he may ask, following Wittgenstein, what rule they are following in their intentional compliance. In either case, the enquiry starts from the subject's own conception of his role in complying with authority. Weber, it is true, appears to be working from the perspective of those having authority, not of their subordinates:

> . . . it is useful to classify the types of authority according to the kind of claim to legitimacy typically made by each. (Weber, 1947, 324)

However, if these claims are to be effective in bringing about compliance, they must be genuinely accepted, not necessarily by those who make them, but by those who are subject to them. It is the subordinates who will need to have some notion of charismatic, traditional, or rational-legal authority (it need not, of course, be a highly articulated notion) if they are to be subordinate to it. And he who obeys is necessarily either acting for some reason, or following a rule of some kind; unless he has some understanding of what the rule is, and some awareness that he is following it, he cannot properly be said to be obeying at all, and we will need a different description of what he is doing. As J.M. Cameron remarks, this is part of the meaning of the concepts of authority and obedience. One who maintains that he is obliged to obey the command of an authority and that no reason need or could be advanced *why* he should obey, maintains what is without sense, and though such expressions as 'blind obedience' and 'unthinking obedience' are used, they are: 'deliberately paradoxical expressions designed to indicate that . . . questions about obedience cannot be raised' (Cameron, in Todd, 1962, 207).

It is true that in some situations, such as in team sports, compliance with a command may need to be so prompt as to leave no time for deliberation at the moment of obeying; but there must previously have been some kind of deliberation, some understanding of the subordinate role of a team member and of its scope, some notion of following a rule, even when the rule is to comply promptly on cue. Of course, not all authoritative communications, even intentional ones, are commands; as we have seen, an authority may make suggestions to be followed, or decisions to be complied with. But even in these cases, where compliance with authority does not involve obedience to a command,

> the concept of authority would be unintelligible unless we first had the concept of following rules with the built-in notion that there are correct or incorrect ways of doing things. (Peters, 1966, 238)

It is the law that makes the king, not vice versa, and more generally, it is the rule that makes the authority. The rules of cricket are prior to the umpire's authority, not merely chronologically, but logically as well, and in a double sense: they prescribe to him rules to be observed in making his decisions, and they prescribe to the players the rule that the umpire's decisions are to be accepted. Even if a particular decision is, through the umpire's inadvertence, not in accord with the rules of cricket, it *is* in accord with the rules of cricket that he should make it, and that the players should abide by it; and an umpire's decision, even a mistaken one, may be called a *ruling*. (Of course, to ask whether an umpire's decision was correct is to ask for reasons of a different kind from asking who should be umpire, or whether the game needs umpires at all, or whether the relevant rule is a good one.)

It is important, however, not to overload the notion of a rule, even in relation to 'rule-governed activities', to the point where reasonable behaviour, tradition, the point of an activity, etc., all become matters of rules. What makes that word inappropriate is its implying that every activity can be reduced to a set of rules, that the rules *constitute* the activity. That is not true even of a game; if it were, then any player who broke a rule would be, quite literally, not playing the game. No doubt some breaches of rules constitute withdrawal from the game, but others do not, and the difference between the two is not always reducible to a set of rules, either. In most cases where an umpire imposes a penalty, the player is breaking a rule, but still playing the old game.

There may, then, be cases when authority is associated with nothing formal enough to be described as a rule or a set of rules, so that Peters is going too far in asserting that notions of authority necessarily involve notions of rule-following. What would seem to be unintelligible would be a notion of authority unrelated to the 'notion that there are correct or incorrect ways of doing things' (Peters, 1966, 238). The latter notion is indeed built into the idea of following a rule, but may also be found built into something less formal, such as the point of an activity, or the standards of reasonable behaviour. There may not be a *rule* governing every instance of authority, but where there is not, there must always be some *reason* for the authority.

As we cannot easily think of authority apart from rules or reasons, so we cannot easily think of authority apart from limits, since a rule will usually involve limits of some kind. If such expressions as 'unlimited authority' (except, perhaps, with reference to God) are to escape self-contradiction, they must be understood as applying within a context of some kind, and the context will set the limits, though there are cases where the limits are so broad as almost to disappear from view, notably under totalitarian governments. Even a sovereign legislature, which Benn offers as an example of an authority without limits (Benn, 1967, I, 215), may have authority to legislate on all matters, but only within a particular country, and according to the legislative procedures currently in force (even if these procedures are themselves subject to change by the same legislature). Likewise an umpire may have unrestricted authority to decide all disputes which arise, but only if they concern the game of cricket, and indeed, only if they concern a particular cricket match.

To understand authority, then, either as participants or as observers, involves understanding some notions of rules and rule-following. Is the converse also true, that the notion of a rule involves the notion of authority, and is unintelligible without it? Clearly it need not involve the authority of an umpire, authorised to make decisions, for some games are played without umpire or referee, so that participants must resolve disputes among themselves. There are then no authoritative rulings, but only agreements. They are, however, agreements about what the rules of the game prescribe and how they are to be applied to a particular situation; for if it is possible to play a game without an umpire, it would make no sense to speak of playing a game without rules, and, if there is no umpire whose authority can be appealed to, the players can still appeal to the authority of the rules. (That is why it is crude to suggest, as Weldon (1953, 56-7) does, that statements about the authority of umpires are nothing more than statements about the penalties which the player risks if he does not abide by the umpire's decisions. Moreover, some players will know these rules better than other players, and even if there is no rule that disputes be referred to these experts for a ruling, or that the other players accept their rulings, they may still be said to have authority in the sense that they are authorities on the rules of the game (see Chapter 5).

If it is in this sense that we read Winch's judgement that between authority and rule

> . . . the connection is conceptual rather than contingent. The acceptance of authority is not just something which, as a matter of fact, you cannot get along without if you want to participate in rule-governed activities; rather, to participate in rule-governed activities *is,* in a certain way, to accept authority (Winch, in Quinton, 1967, 99)

that is, if we take Winch to be talking not solely of the authority of an arbitrator authorised to give rulings, but also of the authority of the expert on the rules, or of the authority of the rules themselves, then it is difficult to dispute his assertion, or to understand why Peters rejects it, and does 'not want to make the sphere of "authority" co-extensive with that of a right and a wrong way of doing things', as Winch does. If, as Peters insists, there are 'other methods of deciding what is right' (Peters, 1966, 246), apart from authoritative methods, it is not obvious what they could be, excluding not only the authority of the arbitrator, but also the authority of the expert, or of the rule. Indeed, if a complaint lies against Winch, it may be that his making 'the sphere of "authority" co-extensive with that of a right and a wrong way of doing things' is, in the way he does it, true by definition and uninteresting, rather than that it is false, as Peters suggests.

Nor is it obvious, as Peters asserts, that:

> We can conceive of a society of highly moral beings living together amicably out of respect for the moral law and for each other as rational beings, without anyone being in authority, and without anyone being thought of as an authority (Peters, 1966, 238)

if he is asserting anything more than a logical possibility. It is true, presumably, that highly moral beings would not need to be coerced into virtuous conduct. But virtuous conduct is, in many situations, authority-following conduct. A virtuous and rational football player will not think it beneath him to comply with the referee's rulings; on the contrary, his compliance will be prompt and complete, and he will never need to be threatened with penalties. Moreover, unless these beings agree to foreswear all activities requiring co-operation among themselves, they will have a practical need, if not a logical need, for authorities of other kinds, to co-ordinate their common endeavours. Even rational oarsmen will row better if one of their number is designated as the stroke, and the others row in time with him. And though an orchestra, with far more members and a far greater variety of operations to be co-ordinated, can certainly be thought of without a conductor, in practice all orchestras have conductors, and play better if they have conductors. To ascribe this need for conductors to the shortcomings of musicians as rational and moral beings might be thought offensive, and is in any event unnecessary: it is simply more effective if all the musicians follow the conductor than if each one tries to follow his neighbour. Nor need we follow Sinyavsky's Russian secret policeman in his belief that the only reason why they will play the same tune is that the conductor is forcing them to do so (Sinyavsky, 1960, 25).

Emphasis on rules, and on a right way of doing things, has led some writers on authority to deny that, in following authority, one is subject to the will of another. Friedrich speaks of authority as 'a quality of communication, rather than of persons' (*Nomas I*, 1958, 35-6), and Winch asserts that 'the authoritative character of an individual's will derives from its connection with the idea of a right way of doing things', so that 'authority cannot be understood as a peculiar sort of influence of one will upon another'. 'Authority is not a sort of influence. It is not a kind of *causal* relation between individual wills but an *internal* relation'. Winch is insisting, almost to the point of paradox, that the norm makes the authority. and that if the authority is followed, it is followed for the sake of the norm: rules rule. He is also insisting that 'the very notion of a human will, capable of deliberating and making decisions' makes it impossible to think of command-and-obedience as cause-and-effect (Quinton, 1967, 98-9). If someone jumps overboard at my command, my command is not the *cause* of his getting wet, as my push would have been the cause if I had simply thrown him overboard.

A person pushed or thrown is an object, whose movement is caused, that is, physically necessitated. A person commanded, and obeying the command, is a subject. Even if he jumps instantly on cue ('blind obedience'), he must previously have set himself to do so, by a decision, of some kind, to follow the rule: obey instantly the commands of X. It may, of course, be folly on his part, even base folly, to accept for himself a subordination too extensive, or to an authority obviously unworthy, but *he* has accepted it. That being the case, obedience always involves an additional decision on the part of the subject, so that a command cannot be a cause, as a push can.

An apparent exception to all this is an instantaneous response to an abruptly uttered order. A barked command 'Jump!' may be instantly complied with by one or two people in a group; but then, the same word *jump* may also be used to refer to the quite involuntary starting which is the response of all members of the group when startled by a sudden sound, and they would not then be obeying a command. If a response is involuntary, or nearly so, then it is a reaction experienced by a person rather than an action which he performs, so that questions of human obedience and the reasons for it do not arise. They would arise, of course, if a member of the group attempted to bring his involuntary response under conscious control, anticipating the stimulus and setting himself to respond to it, or not to respond, intentionally. And there may be intermediate cases when it is hard to tell whether the movement of a person who is ill, drugged, sleepy, or very passive should be understood as an involuntary response, or as a voluntary act in obedience to an authority.

It might seem that the kind of authority called charismatic would be difficult to fit into this insistence on the subordination of authority to reasonings or rules. Charismatic authority, we are told, is authority personal to the holder of it, for if it rested on rules, it would no longer be charismatic authority, but traditional or rational-legal authority, so that expressions like 'routinised charisma' have an unsatisfactory element of paradox about them: what is essentially irregular, cannot be regularised without changing its nature. And a person having this kind of authority with his followers does not, we are told, offer them reasons why they should follow him, for they believe him to be an exceptional person who need not give reasons. But even here the priority of rules or reasons over authority holds. His followers would find unintelligible his authority, and their subordination to it, unless they already had notions of, say, divine favour, exceptional knowledge, and so on. It may be thought inappropriate, even improper, to ask an exceptional person to give reasons for his pronouncements; but he could not be recognised as such without reasons of some kind. There must be some way of identifying an authoritative utterance; and it cannot be the content, since to judge the utterance on the merits of its content is not to follow it as authoritative. Rather, there must be a public means of recognising it as authoritative, or as Hobbes put it, '. . . marks, whereby a man may discern in what man, or assembly of men, the sovereign power is placed and resideth' (*Leviathan*, 18).

To say that authority can be understood only in terms of rules and reasons, is not to say that these rules and reasons must be recapitulated on the occasion of every authoritative utterance. This is clearest when the authoritative utterance is a command; for commands are a class of regulatory utterances in which reasons are normally neither offered nor asked for. A person receiving a command can enquire whether it emanates from a person who has authority to give it, and is not exceeding his competence; but if it passes such tests, this constitutes the only justification the command can have, as command, and there is no point in asking for further justification. But behind every authoritative command, however curtly uttered, lies what Friedrich calls 'the capacity for reasoned elaboration'. Such reasoned elaboration, he explains, will be entirely 'in terms of the opinions, values, beliefs, interests and needs of the community within which the authority operates' (Friedrich, 1963, 226; *Nomos I,* 1958, 29).

Rules, too, and right-ways-of-doing-things, may have no very exalted status in the eyes of an observer who does not share them but comments on them from the outside, noting that the reasoned elaboration of the participants may appear quite irrational to a non-participant. The rules may be no more than the rules of a game, having no authority outside the circle of players. There may be a right way of doing something of no great importance, and of interest only to a few. Every authority, then, will be thought to be supported, as Hume believed that public authority was supported, by the opinion of those subject to it (Hume, 1953, 24), whether that opinion is well-founded or ill-founded.

Legal authority will serve as an example to illustrate this approach to authority, and the difficulties that it runs into. Legislatures and legislators, courts and judges, precedents, jurisconsults, and the law itself may all be said, in various senses, to have authority, and our understanding of law involves these heterogeneous kinds of authority, some less amenable than others to a positivist account of law as command and enforcement. At first sight the authority of a court seems to fit readily into the positivist picture: it is true in one obvious sense that 'the law is what the courts say it is', that is to say, what the appropriate court declares in a particular case about rights and obligations *is* what those rights and obligations are in law, and the decision is authoritative *because* it has been made by the appropriate court. But there is more to be said. The court does not see itself as creating and negating rights and obligations, *auctor ac subversor suarum legum,* but as declaring what they are: we speak of the *finding* of a court. Even legislatures have not always been thought of as creating legal rights and obligations where none existed before; a medieval parliament, like a modern court, was seen rather as finding and declaring the law, as giving a decision on existing legal rights and obligations in the course of resolving a case in dispute; but where modern legislatures are under no such constraint, and are thought of as competent to create legal rights and obligations, courts are not. Hence a court may be said to *reverse* a previous decision which was *mistaken,* but such language would be inappropriate if applied to the activity of a legislature in amending or repealing existing law (Robison, in Harris, 1976, 115-16). 'The law is what the courts say it is', but, as Hart adds:

> . . . any individual judge coming to his office . . . finds a rule . . . established as a tradition and accepted as the standard for the conduct of that office. This circumscribes, while allowing, the creative activity of its occupants . . . The adherence of the judge is required to maintain the standards, but the judge does not make them. (Hart, 1961, 142)

Judges, then, like umpires, have authority, sometimes final authority, to make decisions in accordance with the appropriate rules; unlike umpires, they sometimes explain their decisions at length, giving reasons why some precedents rather than others must be taken as authoritative in the case at hand, why the law required the court to decide as it did. Such explanation, it may be thought, adds nothing to the authoritativeness of the court's decision, and 'the competent court', that is, the court within whose sphere the case in question falls, will decide authoritatively even if it is presided over by a judge who is very *in*competent at legal reasoning. If the court's decision is said to be mistaken, this need not mean, and usually will not mean, that it had no authority to decide the case. The Supreme Court of the United States was competent to decide the case of *Minersville School District v. Gobitis,* even though that decision was subsequently reversed, and the legal reasoning associated with it was rejected, by the same court in *West Virginia Board of Education v. Barnette* (310 U.S., 586; 319 U.S., 624). But the authority which belongs to a judge by virtue of his office may be augmented by authority in another sense, the sense associated with men of learning, if his judgements are well argued; and the practice of explaining the reasons for court decisions bears witness to the widespread and longstanding desire so to augment, with the authority of scholarship, the authority *ex officio* of courts and their judgements.

Moreover, courts need to be deferred to, if their awards are to be complied with, for they themselves seldom control the means to enforce their own decisions. Even here the account of law as command and enforcement is cruder and simpler than reality; for if the decision of a court is enforced, this is normally done by the executive arm of government, not by the court. In order for the court's decision to be enforced, there must first be unforced compliance with it by the executive, either pleased by the direction of the verdict or persuaded by the court's reasoning or in awe of the court's *auctoritas.*

Reasoning which is associated with judicial decisions is often taken to be an excellent example of reasoning within the framework of a specific body of rules, those of the body of law within which the court operates. The more closely such a body of rules is followed, the more closely reasoned judicial decisions can be; conversely, to interpret more broadly, as in the United States, the role of the judiciary and the rules it is to follow, is to run the risk of more loosely argued judicial decisions at best, and at worst of a blurring of the distinction, so important to the authority of the courts and the law, between the decisions of the courts and the personal opinions of judges. In this connection, the legal reasoning of the Supreme Court of Victoria in *Watt v. Rama* (Victorian Reports, 1972, 353-82) may be compared with that of the United States Supreme Court in *Roe v. Wade* (410 U.S., 113-78). The latter scarcely reads like the pronouncement of a court at all. But the law is too varied in its content, and in particular its moral content is too clearly ineradicable, for it to function as a self-contained body of rules and procedures, within which legal reasoning takes place; for if law can, for some purposes, be thought of as enclosed within the boundaries of a particular jurisdiction, morality clearly cannot. Accordingly, legal reasoning is sometimes evaluation by reference to rules, and sometimes the evaluation of the rules, and the latter can no more be avoided than the former.

What is true of legal authority is also true of authority more generally. If the rules themselves are subjected to evaluation; if any particular set of rules is thought to be amenable to rational attack or defence; if it is suggested that authority must be associated, not merely with reasoning, but with reasonableness, then the argument is very much altered. At this point the writing on authority is full of ambiguity. If the adjective *legitimate* is applied to authority by Weber or anyone else, it sometimes means rightful, sometimes rule-governed, sometimes merely accepted. The *validity* or *effectiveness* of reasoning in support of an authority some-times refers to its soundness, sometimes to its compatability with a given rule, and sometimes merely to its persuasiveness. *Approved* sometimes means 'worthy of approval by humanity', and sometimes merely 'approved' (it is not always made clear by whom, or how strongly, or how we know). And *authority* loses its claim to non-evaluative status, since it sometimes refers to the fact of compliance, according to reasonings the soundness of which need not, and perhaps cannot, be examined, and sometimes to a right to compliance, according to sound reasoning, *recta ratio,* Reason. To say that no one can obey without having a reason for obeying, is not to say that he must always have a good reason. To say that complying with authority is always following a rule, is not to say that it must always be a sensible rule. But even when a person is following silly rules for bad reasons, *he* is following: and to follow is in some measure to be active. A subject is not an object.

5 AUTHORITY AND KNOWLEDGE

Knowledge may give rise to authority. Strong evidence or argument may be said to 'compel assent', and such compulsion has nothing to do with coercion, or even with command. When our minds recognise a proposition as self-evidently true, we are agreeing, not doing, assenting, not obeying. An idea may have a compelling power which is intrinsic to it, and owes nothing to the source from which we received it. Even if we have had evidence or argument placed before us by another person, we may not consider that we are subjecting ourselves to him or obeying him when we assent, but rather, that we are accepting the evidence or the argument itself.

So authority can be ascribed to knowledge and to branches of knowledge; a dictionary or a map may be called authoritative; and a person may be called an authority on something that he knows about. Practical knowledge, knowing how to do something, can also be associated with authority, as when a musician's performance is called *authoritative.* These senses of authority are related rather than identical, for a book, an author and a body of knowledge cannot be authoritative in exactly the same sense, and their relation merits further enquiry. Truth, knowledge, science, the law, or a written text, may all be called authoritative, but they cannot speak for themselves if an enquirer puts further questions to them. Even a written text is dumb in dialogue; it cannot explain its own meaning. In matters of knowledge, passive authorities (as they may be called) can speak only through active authorities: science speaks through scientists, the law speaks through courts and history speaks through historians (but not normally through a single historian, so that the fictional professor of history who answers the telephone with the words 'History speaking', is intentionally ridiculous (Amis, 1954). The hope, associated with Bentham, that complete codification of the law could make it possible to apply law directly to fact, dispensing largely with the mediation of advocates and judges, has nowhere been fulfilled, and it is hard to see how it could be.

For however exhaustively the laws are written down, the task of matching the appropriate legal rule to the facts of a particular case cannot be done in advance. A role always remains for living authorities, for Bentham's 'judge and company'.

When a dictionary is relied on as authoritative, its author may be taken to be an authority on the language; the book, we may be told, cannot be more authoritative than the author who wrote it. But if either the book or its author is called into question, appeal lies to the knowledge which is the source of the authority of book and author alike. The mountain is where it is, whatever the map or the cartographer say. And though it is not always so straightforward to trace the descent of authoritativeness, the direction is always the same. An authoritative pronouncement may give us good reasons for believing that what has been said is true, but an authoritative pronouncement can never make it true, in the way that an authoritative command or decision in law may make something legal. In this respect, scholarly authority is non-official and non-institutional, and so De George can say that 'it would be tempting to call this authority "personal"', and Polanyi can observe that it 'is attached not so much to offices as to persons' (Harris, 1976, 78; Polanyi, 1946, 34). Certainly it is only personal excellence, and not the holding of any institutional office, that makes someone an authority on his subject, to call him an authority is to say that he knows it well or does it well. In another respect, however, nothing could be less personal, nothing more public than the authority of one who knows, for he must always be able to give reasons for his pronouncements, to refer back to the knowledge on which, and by virtue of which, he is an authority. An expert need not give the reasons for his pronouncements – indeed, he is most clearly functioning as an authority when he makes pronouncements without giving reasons, and if he were to communicate his reasons in full at the time, then it would no longer be on his authority that his pronouncements were accepted. But though the reasons need not be given at the time, there must be reasons which could be given, and however well he can formulate them, they are not *his* reasons.

This suggests that the authority of those who know is

somehow more dispensable than the authority of orchestral conductors or the leaders of rescue teams which require co-ordinated efforts. In these cases, only one person can be the director, and the others, however capable, must follow his lead. But once we have worked through a proof or examined the evidence for ourselves, then not merely have we no further need of an authority as the reason for our belief; rather, it is no longer possible to accept it on the authority of someone else, for we have become authorities ourselves. Adjectives like *provisional* and *substitutional* are applied to the authority that is associated with learning. Some go further, speaking, as Peters does, of an 'incompatibility' between authority and science, though he turns out to mean no more than that in academic matters 'reasons must be given' rather than 'originators or umpires produced', and that no authoritative pronouncement can make a statement true (Peters, 1966, 240, 261; Quinton, 1967, 95). But liberal sentiments have often been associated with low views of learned authority and strong language against it. Locke tells us that it cannot increase our knowledge: 'The floating of other men's opinions in our brain makes us not one jot the more knowing, though they happen to be true', and he is forever scoffing at 'reverenced propositions', as Mill is forever scoffing at 'received opinions' (though Mill does not always succeed in allaying the reader's suspicion that he would have less objection to received opinions if they coincided with his own). (Locke, 1961, 158; Mill, *On Liberty*, II; Cowling, 1963.) Knowledge, according to their account of it, is the achievement of solitary men. Propositions accepted on another person's authority may merit the name of true opinion; they can scarcely be called knowledge.

Authority is always associated with inequality of some kind, and nowhere is this more obvious than in the authority that goes with knowledge. In knowing *how* as well as in knowing *about,* some people know more than others. It is often rational to defer to the judgement of those who know more than we do, and irrational to prefer our own judgement. It is often the easiest way, and sometimes the only way, in which we can escape from our own ignorance or incapacity. This is most obvious in childhood. We may sometimes be led, on the authority of our elders, to make mistakes in grammar and pronunciation; but unless we took them in general as authorities on our first language, we could never learn to speak it. Certainly at this stage of learning, 'cognitive do-it-yourself recipes' (Bell, 1971, 192) are profoundly misleading.

An authority in a practical activity is a person who combines knowing how with knowing about it. In learning such an activity, counsel and command run together, and a music student or an apprentice craftsman receives instruction, in part, by receiving instructions. Even in studies that are more academic, this blurring of counsel and command may be observed. At the most advanced stages of study some of the students will become authorities themselves. But the practice of a science involves doing things as well as believing things, and Polanyi has reminded us of the importance of personal contact and influence even among the most eminent natural scientists. Rutherford's own students included four Nobel laureates, Rutherford himself was a student of J.J. Thomson, and in practice

> . . . a full initiation into the premises of science can be gained only by the few who possess the gifts for becoming independent scientists, and they usually achieve it only through close personal association with the intimate views and practice of a distinguished master . . . A master's daily labours will reveal these to the intelligent student and impart to him also some of the master's personal intuitions by which his work is guided. (Polanyi, 1946, 29-30)

Rather than disappearing, our dependence on authority takes other forms as we become more knowledgeable. No one can be knowledgeable in more than one or two spheres. Within these spheres, everyone is dependent on learned authorities in the manner mentioned by Polanyi, even at the most advanced levels of his apprenticeship, accepting conclusions and following procedures before he has fully understood the reasons for them. Outside these spheres he can never hope to understand the reasons fully, and must necessarily rely on the relevant authorities. A young archaeologist may be dependent in one way, if he is to learn his craft, on the authoritative judgements of senior archaeologists whose reasoning he may eventually come to understand fully, and even to improve upon. He may be dependent in another way, in such matters as Carbon-14 dating, on the authoritative judgements of physicists whose reasoning he may never understand, and never need to understand. Thus scholars, whose craft is often thought to make them the most autonomous of men, are far from being solitary cultivators of the garden of knowledge, appropriating bits of it as their own by mixing the labour of their reflections with the data which their senses apprehend. Rather, they are elevated and sustained by a network of other men's authoritative judgements which it is pointless to ignore or deny. 'We are dwarves standing upon the shoulders of giants', Bernard of Chartres is supposed to have said (Southern, 1962, 211), affirming both the scholar's ascendancy over his predecessors and his dependence on them. Only by relying on authority in matters of knowledge can anyone become a learned authority himself (and even then, only on very few subjects); only by relying on authorities whose competence he is not yet competent to assess, will he ever come to be competent to assess it. If they are sufficiently incompetent, of course, he may never know, but he has no alternative to taking that risk.

A person becomes an authority on any subject solely by virtue of his knowledge of it. Authority in this sense is not bestowed, delegated, revoked, and so on. For a research laboratory to appoint a man as its director is to bestow on him authority in the sense to be considered in Chapter 8: a certain scope for decision and command. But the appointment cannot make him an authority on his subject. In this respect, learned authority resembles *de facto* authority, the sense of the word considered in Chapter 3: learned authority is specific to its subject, and normally an authority on a subject is accepted by those who know that subject, as knowing even more than they do.

But while *de facto* authority rests on nothing more than its subordinates' beliefs, true or false, so that there can be no such thing as spurious authority, a person is a learned authority by virtue of his learning, not of his acceptance. If a charlatan is exposed as such, we do not say that he was formerly an authority on what he was thought to know about, but has now ceased to be an authority on it; we say that he was never an authority, but merely pretended to be, and was mistakenly believed to be, that his authority was spurious and not genuine. It is an inescapable practical difficulty with learned authority that the learned know best who the learned are, while those who know a subject less well will also be less reliable in their judgements about who the best authorities are.

As authority in the sense considered in Chapter 8 is sometimes spoken of as a right to issue commands, so learned authority is sometimes spoken of as a right to make pronouncements, to offer counsel, or to teach (Peters, 1966, 239; Harris, 1976, 87). This symmetry is attractive, but it involves difficulties. We understand talk of rights partly by considering how they might be exercised. If those who know have a right to make pronouncements, it is not always obvious what the corresponding obligations are, not always obvious who is obliged, and to do what: to consult, to listen, to believe, and so on. In particular cases this may be clear enough. An inexperienced surgeon may be obliged, before undertaking an unfamiliar operation, to consult someone who knows more about it, and to attend very closely to his counsel. (Such knowledge of the likely consequences of some action that he is contemplating, is not *moral* knowledge in the sense considered in Chapter 6, but rather what Hughes calls 'pre-moral knowledge' (Hughes, 1978, 30-1). Without it, he will lack something that he needs in order to make his moral decision.) In the same way, a lecturer, unsure about a piece of information, may be obliged to consult an authoritative work of reference. He is obliged because it is his business to find out what he needs to know, if he does not know it already. And though for any person '. . . it may well be the part of wisdom and of prudence to utilise the knowledge of the learned in relevant ways' (Harris, 1976, 87), it is hard to see that he has any obligation to do so unless he has an obligation to acquire the knowledge that the learned authority or the authoritative work of reference can provide. A right to make pronouncements would seem pointless if nobody is obliged to attend to them. Moreover, it may not even be possible to make pronouncements unless the authoritative person has access to research funds, equipment, materials and means of publicity; and until it is specified whose obligation it is to provide him with these necessities, and in what quantity, we will not know how we should understand a right to make pronouncements, if such a right is ascribed to him.

A book may be called authoritative even if those who consult it make no use of the information they find there, and a person may be an authority on a subject even if the advice he gives is not followed. We seek medical *advice,* and legal *counsel.* (We also speak of doctors' *orders,* but a doctor, however peremptory his manner, has no obvious rights of command over his patients, and they would seem to have no obligation to act on his advice apart from any obligation they may have to take care of their health and life.) Learned authority answers the question, 'Why should I agree or believe?' and not the question, 'Why should I obey?'

Plato, to be sure, has usually been understood to hold that knowledge not merely constitutes its holder an authority on what he knows about but also confers on him a right to issue commands, and to be obeyed; that those who know should also be those who decide and command. Even Aristotle observes, in passing, that there is something inappropriate in the subordination of one who is wiser to the commands of one who is less wise (Aristotle, *Metaphysics,* 982a). More recently, however, it has become customary to minimise, or to reject altogether, connections between those two senses of authority, learned authority and a right to command. Even in research insitutes it is not usually thought necessary that the most learned person in any department should be the executive head of it. In practical matters there is frequently a need for prompt decision, a common policy, co-ordinated effort; but scholarship, it may seem, is in no hurry, and has need only for the consultative authority of learning, not for the executive authority of command or binding decision.

On the other hand, scholarship is not carried on entirely by individual scholars who ask one another's advice and communicate their findings to one another face to face. Scholars are trained in instiutions of learning, and communicate their ideas through academic journals, conferences, and so on. In these institutions practical considerations cannot be avoided. There are decisions to be made, concerning appointments of staff, the award of scholarships, the construction of programmes of study, the choice of articles for publication, and so on.

Many of these matters involve decisions by which other people are affected, rather than commands which they must obey. The relevant committee determines which of several applicants will be appointed, and the editors determine which of several articles will be published. Their decisions are not commands, properly speaking: unsuccessful candidates are not commanded to do anything, they are simply not appointed; unsuccessful authors are not commanded to do anything, their writings are simply not published.

Clearly the authority to make these decisions must be distinguished, in the person who holds it, from his being an authority on some branch of knowledge. The former is institutional. It is conferred on him, according to the procedures of the institution. According to those rules, it has a term, after which it expires. None of this is true of learned authority. Moreover, his executive authority as editor or director originates in his having been appointed to his office, not in his learning, and an appointee without learning, or without much learning, would be editor or director nonetheless, exercising editor's or director's executive authority. But in practice he will not be able to exercise it well without sufficient learning, for he will be less able to make sound judgements; moreover, if it is widely believed, among those affected by his decisions, that he has not sufficient learning to support sound judgements, his decisions may not win ready acceptance.

To appoint very learned men to these positions of executive authority in academic institutions may be expected to make for *fewer* mistaken decisions, but cannot be expected to guarantee that there will be no mistaken decisions. The best writings may not in every instance be selected for publication, the best courses for approval, or the best candidates for appointment. Valuable work may remain unrecognised and unknown, because unpublished, if those who make editorial decisions find it too novel, or, in some fields, not novel enough. The emergence of more satisfactory explanations in the sciences may be delayed, or original but unsound ideas lent an unmerited respectability, through the mistaken decisions of those in office in academic institutions. But the offices are no more dispensable than the institutions. Scholars must be trained, teachers and research workers certified, a selection made of reports and articles to be published, swift and reliable contact among people in the same branch of knowledge facilitated. Without decisions made about the selection of materials for publication, the content of a course of study in each subject and the appropriate persons to teach it, there could be no training of new adepts, and the subject would soon become extinct. Even those whose insights or discoveries have transformed a field of knowledge have needed, in nearly every instance, first to be trained in it; and in every case without exception they need a body of people trained in a common tradition to receive their new insights or discoveries into that tradition, and to qualify, correct, enlarge upon, and communicate them. These things can be done only in institutions, and by means of making decisions, and someone has to be designated to make them (Polanyi, 1946, 30-40).

This executive authority within institutions of learning must be distinguished very sharply from the main subject of the present chapter, that is, the sense of *authority* in which a person is said to be an authority on his subject, a work of reference to be authoritative, or a musician to play authoritatively. Such authority is not institutional; no one is appointed to be an authority on his subject, and in that sense it is sometimes said to be personal, and to require personal excellence. But it is impersonal, too, for it refers us back constantly from the person to the body of knowledge on which, and by virtue of which, he is an authority, and if it becomes apparent that he is not the master of this body of knowledge, his standing as an authority on it is destroyed. It is a sense of the word whose meaning is not easily rendered in the language of rights and duties. Authority in this sense is associated with tutelage and dependence, and its importance has been minimised by those who see the acquisition and the advancement of knowledge solely as the activity of individual persons. But from the most elementary stages of learning to the most advanced, from the child learning his first language to the postgraduate student, to be a learner is to be attached to another person who is already engaged in the activity which the neophyte is learning.

Even those who themselves become authorities on their subjects have achieved this by leaning heavily, even at the most advanced levels of their studies, on the authority of those whom they in their turn may surpass and supplant as authorities.

6 MORAL AUTHORITY

Some people may know more than others about a body of rules. To be an authority on a body of rules would seem to be a straightforward instance of the kind of authority considered in Chapter 5, with no obvious additional difficulties. Thus an expert on the present rules of tennis, or on the history of the rules of chess, is an ordinary learned authority. Again, no obvious difficulties arise if the knowledge is of moral rules, provided that the authority takes up a standpoint outside of those rules. Thus an anthropologist may be an authority on the rules observed, or honoured, as moral rules by the Bushmen. And where a sociologist is himself a member of the group he is studying, as when he is an authority on the values (as he will probably call them) of sociologists, he will usually make some effort to set himself at a distance from them.

But the suggestion that there can be authorities on what is right, rather than merely on what someone else believes to be right, is likely to encounter resistance. Authority, it may be said, is simply out of place in matters of right and wrong. Clearly a positivist, or anyone else who thinks that moral beliefs fall outside the sphere of knowledge, must also hold that there can be no authorities on the validity of moral beliefs. For if good and bad are entirely in the eye of the beholder, if all evaluative statements are merely expressions of feelings in the person who makes them, then normally nobody will know more about his feelings than he does, nobody will be able to speak of them more authoritatively than he can. If, on the other hand, there can be *knowledge* of right and wrong, then it is likely that, as in other areas of knowledge, some people will know more than others, and it will be proper to call such people authorities, and to speak of them as authorities in the sphere of morality, moral authorities.

But there are other kinds of authority which may easily be mistaken for moral authority. For instance, utilitarians hold that what is good to do is what will make people happy, and some utilitarians may also hold, as Austin did, that as long as most people do not know what will maximise happiness, their moral conduct and their happiness will depend upon their being prepared to 'trust on authority' the moral rules proposed to them by 'the comparative few, who study the science assiduously'. Among those few, he believed, there were no moral disputes incapable of being resolved by 'scientific enquiry', so that they would speak authoritatively with one voice (Austin, 1954, 73-82; Friedman, in Schneewind, 1969, 379-425).

To Austin, one of the comparative few who study the science assiduously, is simply a person who knows more than others know about the most effective means of promoting happiness. That is the science he studies assiduously. His expertise does not lie in his identifying of good conduct with happiness-producing conduct, and it is hard to see how there could be expertise in making that identification, central to the utilitarian moral position. His authority, then, is not a *moral* authority, but an ancillary expertise in ways and means of making people happy.

But if we turn from Austin to Aristotle, we find an account of an authority which is morally central. The importance of moral authority is energetically asserted by Aristotle:

> a powerfully built man who has been blinded trips and falls heavily as he moves about, because he is unable to see. Well, it happens like that in morals; if we don't have a guide, we stumble. (Aristotle, *Nichomachean Ethics,* 1144b)

Indeed, he even observes that a good choice is the choice a virtuous man would make (Aristotle, *Nichomachean Ethics,* 1139a). If he had said that a good wall is a wall built by a good bricklayer, or that a good geography book is a book written by a good geographer, the statement would have seemed pointless; but the statement that a good choice is the choice a virtuous man would make, for some reason does not seem similarly pointless. Perhaps goodness is more readily recognised in a good man than in a good ethical argument. Whatever the reason for it, the authority of the *phronimos,* the man of practical wisdom, has an important place in Aristotle's ethical argument. The *phronimos* is a practical authority; not a man who knows something in theory, but a man who can do something in practice, just as 'we are not rendered any more capable of healthy and athletic activities by any knowledge we may have of medicine and physical training' (Aristotle, *Nichomachean Ethics,* 1143b). His excellence shows itself, not primarily in his knowledge of general principles, but more in his capacity to deliberate wisely and to make sound moral judgements, and that capacity, Aristotle believes, comes only with experience (Aristotle, *Nichomachean Ethics,* 1141b, 1142a). The less experience we have had, the more we will need to seek moral counsel: most clearly in childhood, but in later life too, particularly if we are confronted by unfamiliar choices or unaccustomed strains. We will consult a moral authority, not seeking novelties, nor commands, nor primarily for the sake of arguments, but for the sake of sound judgements. We will ask him, not 'Why should I behave virtuously?' (for we may often know that as well as he does), but rather 'Would this action, in these circumstances, be compatible with virtuous conduct?', or even, as Baier suggests, 'What would you do in my place?' (Baier, 1965, 10). This is a sensible question to ask him, if he is a man of great intelligence, experience and practical wisdom which we can draw upon; for it is our aim to make a good choice, and a good choice is the choice that a virtuous man would make.

There would be no point in calling someone a good judge of anything, unless there were some way of verifying his judgements. Judgements of speeds and distances, or of race-horses, may readily be verified, so that it is easy to tell who is a good judge in these matters. The verification of moral judgements is certainly less straightforward, so that there is more room for disagreement over whose judgement is more reliable. To concede, however, that there is *any* means of verifying *any* moral judgement is to concede that there may be moral authorities in the sense considered by Aristotle.

Clearly moral judgement, unlike Mycenean archaeology, is not the kind of field in which it would make sense to demand a list of the best ten authorities on earth; but that does not mean that no one's moral judgement is any better than anyone else's.

Following Aristotle, then, it is possible to think of moral

authority without imagining that moral knowledge is restricted to a series of propositions about right and wrong (moral knowledge may still be held to include propositional knowledge). We may then think of moral authority chiefly as a capacity to make sound judgements in moral matters, together, perhaps, with habits of acting on those judgements. If we associate such moral authority with knowledge, we may think of it as more like knowing a city well than like knowing a fact, more like being a good judge of racehorses than like having an accurate memory for racing results, more like being a skilful diagnostician or surgeon than like being an able student of anatomy. But non-propositional knowledge, too, is unevenly distributed. If some people are better informed, more experienced, more discriminating, more intelligent, or more sensitive in moral matters than we are, then there seems to be no reason why we should not take them as authorities, for precept or example or both, in the hope that we may learn to judge as they judge, and to do as they do. Indeed, we may consider that we are bound to take them as authorities; for though we may have no obligation to consult a learned authority unless it is our business to acquire some piece of knowledge, it would be odd for anyone to maintain that knowledge of right conduct is none of his business, that he is free to take it or leave it. If there are moral authorities, it seems that we may be morally bound to attend to them.

It is possible, in deciding what to believe about some matter (a technical matter, perhaps), to make no investigation oneself but to rely entirely on the judgement of another person. Some, however, would consider such a procedure inappropriate in the case of moral beliefs. They would insist that it is not enough for a moral belief to be true, or supported by valid reasoning, but that it must also be in some way appropriated as his own by each person who holds it, so that he sees for himself the rightness or wrongness of each of the things that he believes to be right or wrong. If he does not, we are told, 'authenticity' or 'autonomy' have passed him by. But it may sometimes be rational, even in one's own moral conduct, to rely heavily on another person's judgement without hearing in full the reasons for that judgement, or without fully accepting those reasons. An alcoholic, knowing his own judgement to be impaired, may begin his own rehabilitation by following 'blindly' the judgement of another person. But his action cannot be genuinely blind, for if it were, he would have no reason for holding another person's judgement to be more dependable than his own. Moreover, beliefs about one's own moral obligations are practical: one believes that one is bound to *act*, and not merely to believe, in a certain way. And anyone who acts on moral advice is himself acting; anyone who decides to follow a moral authority is himself deciding. Whatever counsel he listens to, it is he who must eventually act, and that is the end of listening to counsel. At the point of deciding, everyone alike decides for himself, the obedient deciding to obey no less than the disobedient decides to disobey, the follower of advice no less than the ignorer of advice. In this sense, everyone alike is morally autonomous, and that is no argument whatever for depriving oneself of the best counsel available, in moral as in technical matters (Anscombe, in Todd, 1962, 179-88).

There may be knowledge of technical matters (knowledge, for instance, of the likely consequences of some action we are contemplating) which we may need to have before we can make an informed moral judgement. If we lack such knowledge, 'pre-moral knowledge', as Gerard Hughes calls it (Hughes, 1978, 30-1), we may consider ourselves obliged to consult a motor mechanic or a physician, not as *moral* authorities, but as authorities on steering gear or heart disease, whose judgement on these matters we believe to be more reliable than our own.

Moral authority can be thought to exist only if we consider someone else's *moral* judgement to be more reliable than our own. It is impossible to rely on such an authority to the exclusion of ordinary moral deliberation; rather, it is relied on as part of a procedure of moral deliberation. To judge that someone else's judgement is more reliable than one's own, is an exercise of one's own judgement. One name for each person's practical judgement in moral matters is conscience, and without that faculty, we could make no judgement about whose moral counsel or example to follow, or how far to follow it. It is the same with memory: without memory, we could make no judgement about past events, but this does not exclude reliance on another person's memory, or on some public record, if we have reason to believe that our unaided memory is less reliable. Similarly,

> . . . any reasonable man knows that what one has conscientiously decided on one may later conscientiously regret. A man may have reasons to judge that another man's moral counsel is more reliable than his own unaided conscience; he will in any case be well advised to take counsel with others; he may, moreover, have reasons to believe that some public source of moral teaching is more reliable than his own unaided judgement. Of course he would not have any basis for such judgement if he did not already rely on his own moral judgements to some extent but it would be sophistical to argue from this that his own conscience must after all be for him the last word about what he ought to do. (Anscombe, in Todd, 1962, 183-4)

Even in scholarship, where originality is sometimes to be achieved, it is properly an outcome of an activity whose aim is not originality but understanding; to *seek* originality is narcissistic and out of place. In moral matters it is no more appropriate. My moral judgements are mine, not because they are different from yours, but only because I have made them, and my moral reasoning is mine only in the sense that I have accepted it.

Moreover, to say that someone's conduct is 'autonomous' is not the same thing as saying that it is good, nor does the former imply the latter. Consequently, there is no impropriety in describing an action as reckless, cowardly, intemperate, or whatever – but 'autonomous'.

Emphasis on moral 'autonomy' also obscures the extent to which moral notions and moral habits are acquired, in part, by elucidation and precept and example. As the greatest scientific innovators once learned by authority the science which they then transformed by their own discoveries, so in morality (with the obvious difference that in morality the coincidence of innovation with improvement is a good deal less dependable than in the natural sciences), moral notions and moral habits are learned before they are improved upon, and learned, in the first stages, during childhood. Every Autonomous Man was once a very non-autonomous child.

And as a child learns incorrect as well as correct speech from his elders, but could never learn to speak at all unless he took them for authorities on the language, so a child may come to reject some of the moral precepts he has been taught, but will do so partly in the light of other precepts he has been taught, and bad example may likewise be rejected by reference to better example. Moral precepts and moral virtues are varied, and it is hard to see how even the most energetic moral innovator could seek to amend more than a few of them at one time. In morality as in other things learned,

> If a child were liable not to believe his teacher, how could it happen that he selected only those things to disbelieve that were in fact untrue? So he needs to be liable to believe his teacher. If he is, he will learn at any rate some truth; by its aid he will eventually be able to reject what he is taught that is false so far as it is important that he should: or so it is to be hoped. (Anscombe, in Todd, 1962, 181-2)

In any event, he has little choice, if he is to learn moral notions.

But learning in moral matters is learning to act as well as to believe, learning by practice to make sound judgements, to do some things and to refrain from doing others. To teach morality is not merely to bring a pupil to accept a number of ethical propositions as true, though that must form part of the instruction; far more, it is to bring a pupil to behave in a certain way (to be kind to animals, for instance), and this will hardly be possible without some right to the pupil's obedience, at some stages in his moral tutelage. To acquire moral notions and habits, then, would seem normally to involve authority in at least three senses: command, precept and example. A single person may combine all three in himself, but they can be distinguished from one another in principle. If it is possible to have propositional knowledge of morality, without being outstandingly virtuous, or conversely, to be outstandingly virtuous without having much propositional knowledge of morality, then the former person, who knows *about* morality, will be one kind of authority, and the latter, who knows *how,* will be another kind of authority on morality. And neither of them may have an office or a role (as a parent, for instance) involving a right to command anyone else. The person learning about morality, on his side, will do so in part, by accepting authoritative theoretical propositions, by following authoritative practical example, or by obeying authoritative commands. If he is doing none of these things, then he must be generating morality entirely from within himself. This seems implausible.

If moral authority is thought to arise from superior knowledge, either knowing-about or knowing-how, then spurious authority will be possible. Pronouncements about morality may be received as authoritative by people who mistakenly believe that the person making them is well-informed, perceptive, discriminating. The practical moral example of a plausible rogue may be followed as authoritative, in the mistaken belief that he is virtuous. In this respect as in some others, moral authority may be compared with the authority that rests on knowledge of other kinds, where authority may be called spurious if the excellence on which it is believed to rest does not exist.

To learn morality would be difficult indeed if it were true, as MacIntyre asserts, that 'In our society the notion of moral authority is no longer a viable one'. But he turns out merely to be making the familar point that the existence of 'an agreed right way of doing things is logically prior to the acceptance of authority as to how to do things', while at the same time asserting that 'in our society' there is no 'accepted rule', no 'established and agreed practices', no 'prior social agreement' about right and wrong, no 'established and shared right way of doing things' (MacIntyre, 1967, 53). To determine, particularly with the aid of such blunt instruments as attitude surveys, how much agreement there is on moral questions, is never easy. But even if it is conceded that there may be as little agreement as MacIntyre says there is, that means only that there is no *agreed* way of doing things; it does not show that there is no *right* way of doing things. Once again, if there is such a thing as knowledge of right and wrong, then anyone who knows more has the authority that goes with superior knowledge, whether or not he is widely recognised as an authority on morals; likewise, ill-informed moral counsel and vicious moral example are spuriously and not genuinely authoritative, even if some consider them well informed and virtuous. And if, as MacIntyre says, no single moral authority is likely to be very widely recognised, such lack of consensus will not destroy moral authority, but will merely divide and diversify and confuse it, making it more difficult to distinguish the genuine from the spurious. Moral examples will continue to be followed as authoritative, but they will be diverse examples. Moral pronouncements will continue to be received with respect as authoritative, but they will speak with a multitude of voices, not with one voice. Lovers of moral diversity, or resolute optimists, may be heartened by such fragmentation of moral precept and example. But the condition of moral 'autonomy', the disappearance of moral authorities, will not obviously have been brought closer in practice, and it is not clear that it is attainable even in principle. Nor is it clear what *moral* point there could be in the demand that we shut ourselves off from wise counsel, if we have reason to believe that wise counsel is available. Such self-reliance in any important non-moral matter would be reckless folly. To conduct ourselves differently in moral matters is not obviously more sensible.

7 RELIGIOUS AUTHORITY

Authority in religion may be expected to take different forms in different religions. In some religions the object of worship is not a single, all-knowing, all-powerful, perfect being, but a number of deities, each one of which must be thought of as limited by the knowledge and the power of the others: none of them can be thought of as all-knowing and all-powerful. The knowledge and the power of Jupiter are great, but not unlimited, and his goodness has very obvious limits. Moreover, he is not the creator, for there is no creator. None the less, the Romans attributed *auctoritas* to the gods, as sources, not so much of rightful command and prohibition, as of endorsement and admonition. Augurs and oracles gave advice and warning. To ignore their pronouncements was to spurn weighty counsel, not to disobey rightful command. It was not lawless, but it was reckless (*Thesaurus Linguae Latinae,* II, vi, 1229, 1230, 1233).

Human authority, too, may be associated with such religious notions, in some of the senses of authority previously considered. The pronouncements of some people may, as a matter of fact, be accepted by their fellows in belief or in conduct. Again, there may be rules according to which the commands or the decisions of certain religious officials are deemed rightful and binding. And again, some people may be authorities on religious myths or on their interpretation, or on the performance of religious ceremonies, that is, they may know more than other people about these myths or ceremonies. The latter is an unexceptional instance of the kind of authority that goes with knowing something, for religious ceremonies, beliefs, writings, and so forth may be the object of knowledge. And in addition to knowing *about* a religion, a person may know *how* to perform certain religious ceremonies, to use techniques of meditation, and so on. As in any other instance of the authority that goes with knowing, it is not a procedure of appointment but a capacity to show or to explain which consitutes someone as an authority; a religious official, on the other hand, is such by virtue of some process of designation or appointment. Spurious authority will mean in the former case an unfounded claim to know, in the latter case an unfounded claim to the appropriate designation or appointment. And however clearly the different kinds of religious authority are distinguished, disputes may still arise over the respective claims of the priest, the learned man, the holy man, and so on.

Divine authority is likely to be conceived of much more broadly where a single being is worshipped who is understood to be all-knowing, all-powerful, without limit, without fault. If it is reckless to ignore the counsel of a minor divinity who knows more than mortals know, it is worse than reckless to ignore counsel if it is offered by a being whose knowledge is believed to have no limits. If that being is also believed to be infinitely good, then his moral pronouncements, if he makes any, will be seen as so authoritative that it is not obvious what would count as a good reason for ignoring them. A creator, moreover, is the most complete of authors: of the authority that has been ascribed to founders and originators, no more complete instance can be conceived of than the authority of a being who is believed to be the author of all that exists. Again, if all authoritative relationships are marked by inequality in some sense, no more complete inequality can be imagined than between creature and creator: 'Where wast thou when I laid the foundations of the earth? Declare, if thou hast understanding', God is represented as saying to Job (*Job* 38:4). And when Christ is referred to in the Latin New Testament as *auctor vitae* (*Acts* 3:15), author of life, that phrase can hardly be read otherwise than as an assertion of his divinity.

With such a conception of God, there can be no authority of any kind which does not in some sense depend on him. It might not seem obvious, then, that religious authority can be distinguished from any other kind of authority, since all authority has this religious aspect. But to believe that the authority of priests and parents and civil rulers and learned men depends alike on the authority of God makes it no more difficult than it would otherwise be to distinguish one from another. And it makes no less sense to say of two authorities that they are authorised directly and independently by God than to say that one of them is authorised by God as the subordinate of the other. Both notions of the relation of religious to civil authority have been held, and a great deal of attention has been given in Christendom to delineating their respective limits, the things that are Caesar's and the things that are God's. To express the question in such terms is to reject the notion that civil authority has no independent scope of its own, that all authority is religious authority.

If God is thought to be the source of a communication to a human being, as in a religion understood by its adherents to be revealed, there can be no doubt about the authoritativeness of such a communication from creator to creature. If, in addition, God is believed to have authorised religious institutions, there can be little doubt about their authoritativeness either. Beran, in seeking to show that all authority springs from the subordinate's consent, asserts that this is so even of religious authority (Beran, 1977, 260). But while it is true that each member of a religious connection may make certain promises when he joins it, he would probably think of religious authority as descending from above, not as arising from below, and of his consent as a recognition of that authority, not as the source of it.

Belief in a divine revelation to man does not necessarily imply belief in any form of human religious authority. A direct divine revelation to each individual person could make any human communication of that revelation, and hence any religious institution or authority, unnecessary. If, however, the creature is communicated with by fellow-creatures, then it would seem necessary to claim some form of divine warrant for the channel of communication. Any particular claim on behalf of an authoritative oral tradition, written text, institution or person may, of course, be rejected as ill-founded or exaggerated, corruptions of a revelation, but to reject them all is to reject the idea of a revealed religion, unless each person is the *direct* recipient of the revelation. To believe that there has been a divine revelation, but that there is no means of establishing its content, no means of resolving disputes about its content or its meaning, would invite the question what point there could be in such a revelation.

So it is that the authoritativeness of one or more of these channels of communication – an oral tradition, a written text, an institution, or a person — is normally thought to be indispensable in a religion believed by its adherents to be revealed. But, though all of them may be considered as authoritative, they cannot play identical and interchangeable roles. A body of teachings believed to have been originally revealed, may be passed orally from person to person over time. Even a religion of the book must be transmitted in this way during the period before the book has been written, unless the original revelation is thought to have been made in written form. Moreover, illiteracy or poverty may make a written text inaccessible to many people, so that the revelation must reach them orally if it is to reach them at all. And, although memory may be more reliable among illiterate people who must rely on it completely, lacking the aid of the written word, every oral account of the same events or doctrines will differ in some measure from every other account, so that the person hearing them will need to reconcile the various accounts that he has heard, if he is to be reasonably sure that he is in touch with the central tradition rather than a particular and atypical account of it. This task of reconciliation he may find unworkably difficult if the differences among them are very great.

Some of these difficulties will not arise if the enquirer can be referred to an authoritative written text. Provided that it has been accurately copied, there will be no need for him to compare a number of different accounts, for there will be a single authoritative source. But that source has itself a source. It may be thought to be divinely inspired, but it has been humanly transmitted. It is a human voice that has declared which texts are divinely revealed and which are not, and what is meant by saying that a text is revealed. And even where there is an undisputed text, disputes may arise over its meaning. Religious writings have been no more free than statutes from variety of interpretation. In all such disputes, legal or religious, the text can play the role of a silent authority, but not that of a living arbitrator; there is no point in addressing a question to it, for it has already said its last word. Disputes which persist will have to be resolved by some other authority, if they are to be resolved at all (and if they cannot be resolved, we are again confronted with the odd notion of a divinely revealed message, the content of which it is perhaps unimportant, and certainly impossible, to determine). Men may agree or disagree in their reading of a text, but there will be no point in asking whether any given reading was the correct one, because there will be no means of answering the question.

There are good reasons, then, why silent authorities are often found in association with speaking authorities, books and traditions with institutions and officials and scholars, just as codified laws have not made courts redundant. It will sometimes be possible to resolve a dispute by reference to scholarly authorities. It is an ordinary task of scholarship to establish a reliable text, free from the corruptions which may have crept into it, and to guide a reader in understanding what it means. In addition to the authority of scholars, there may be institutional religious authority: officials or institutions believed to be empowered to make pronouncements or decisions. Such a speaking authority in religious matters need not, of course, be a religious institution or official. Hobbes holds that the civil sovereign, if he is to be effective in that role, must have the last word in religious disputes too (*Leviathan,* 29). There is nothing novel about including religious matters within the authority of Caesar; in antiquity that was commonplace. What is novel is the suggestion that a single revealed religion be made subject to the government of each of the states where it has adherents. Following Hobbes's approach, there will always be a single authoritative body of religious teaching within any state, but there may well be a quite different body of religious teaching in adjacent states where the same religion is professed. There is no claim that each sovereign is divinely protected from error in deciding how the revelation is to be interpreted; merely that his must be the last word within his territory. His subjects must be prepared to go by the rule *cuis regio, eius religio,* receiving from him a single, undisputed teaching, the content of which they may not object to. It is hard to see that the idea of a religion as revealed can sit easily within Hobbes's framework, since the most obvious advantage of revealed religion would seem to be lost unless it were thought to be true, and Hobbes's sovereign offers finality, a single official version of the divine revelation, but no claim to, and apparent indifference to, the reliability of that official version.

Islam, according to its adherents, is a revealed religion, and provides examples of the interaction of some of the forms of religious authority so far considered. The authority of the one God is seen by Muslims as the source of all religious authority. If Muhammad spoke with authority, the source of that authority was God's revelation to him and God's message through him to his followers. That message, 'the uncreated word of God', was proclaimed with the authority of its divine author (Rahman, 1966, 50). It was not proclaimed in writing: the Koran is thought to have been written down largely, though not completely, in Muhammad's lifetime (Guillaume, 1975, 56), but before this People of the Book acquired their book, Islam had only a speaking authority, Muhammad himself. His example, in word and deed, was held to be authoritative, and apart from the Koran itself, a great number of *Hadiths,* stories of his sayings and doings, were told and written down. Not all of them were authentic. Rahman notes: 'A very large proportion of the Hadiths was judged to be spurious and forged by classical Muslim scholars themselves and was excluded from the six canonical collections . . .' (Rahman, 1966, 64, 47).

Another authoritative souce for Islam, together with the recorded *Hadiths* and the Koran itself, was the consensus (*ijma*) of Muslims (Tritton, 1951, 62). Indeed, consensus may be seen as a higher authority, for it was by the consensus of Muslims that rival *Hadiths,* and even rival interpretations of Koranic texts, were accepted and rejected. But as this consensus was not 'vested in any institution' (Rahman, 1966, 75), it must sometimes have been difficult to decide what was good Islam. The Koran, no doubt, was the final authority; but even that demanded authoritative explanation, silent authority that it was (Guillaume, 1975, 88). In the early Muslim centuries it was much disputed how to weigh relatively the claims of recorded traditions, and of Muslim consensus (Rahman, 1966, 60-1). What was in question was practice more often than doctrine. The central Islamic beliefs, in the unity of God and the prophetic office of Muhammad, were very straightforward, and though more extensive statements of belief, Muslim creeds, were compiled, their role in Islamic worship and religious instruction has been a minor one (Guillaume, 1975, 115, 134): 'From the very beginning . . . there is to be seen a preoccupation with law rather than . . . theology' (Rahman, 1966, 103), and Islam, like Judaism, has been understood by its adherents in legal terms. Hence the importance, as speaking authorities, of Muslim legal scholars, doctors of the law. It was through their spoken consensus that the silent consensus of Muslims was often expressed. Such authority is quite distinct, of course, from the authority in Islam of any institutionalised executive or judicial body, of which the most obvious instance was the Caliphate. The original theory of the Caliphate seems to have been that all Muslims would live under a single Muslim ruler as they had done in Muhammad's lifetime, so that Islam would continue to have a single speaking authority. (Though in practice, even in the earliest years after Muhammad's death, the Caliphate was as much a point of contention among Muslims as a focus of their unity; the great division between Sunni and Shia Muslims began in a dispute over the rightful succession to the Caliphate (Guillaume, 1975, 79ff).) The claims made on behalf of the Caliphate are usually said to have stopped short of inerrancy: the Caliph, Commander of the Faithful, was to have the last word in Islam, and no authority on earth was to be greater than his, but there was not said to be any divine guarantee that his decisions would be right. Sunni Islam 'recognises in the Caliph only a political and religious executive head of the Community', in contrast to the much more extensive claims to inerrancy made on behalf of the Imams of the Shia branch of Islam (Rahman, 1966, 173). There may appear to be some resemblance between the Caliph and Hobbes's sovereign, who also had the last word on all matters, civil and religious alike, but no assurance from God that what is decided in religious matters will be rightly decided. But there are important differences. There was to be a sovereign in every state, but only one Caliph on earth. Moreover, the sovereign was primarily a civil office-bearer, whose religious functions were a branch of his civil functions; he was head of the church because he was head of state, and the church was a state church. The Caliphate, on the other hand, was a religious office first, and the Caliph owed his civil role entirely to his office as Commander of the Faithful.

And though the very distinction between Caesar's things and God's, between civil and religious authority, has received much less attention in Islam than in Christendom, there are discernible differences in principle between the two forms of authority, however difficult it may be to unravel them in practice. Hobbes's civil sovereign is not only a court, but also a legislator, competent to create new rights and obligations, and not bound by his own past pronouncements: what the sovereign has enacted today, the sovereign may repeal tomorrow. Not so with the institutions of a revealed religion. Their office is to protect from confusion and corruption a message and a movement whose source is not the will of a human sovereign, but the unchanging mind of God. It would be incompatible with this understanding of their role to claim for them the authority of a religious legislator, to enact and repeal at their sovereign judgement. Even the Shia Imams, it would seem, must be understood more as maintaining and preserving than as innovating, more as a court (divinely protected, perhaps, from erroneous judgements) than as a legislator.

The relation between a sacred text and a religious institution is closely analogous to the relation between statute law and courts of law. The courts are not the source of statute law, which originates elsewhere. Rather, the role of courts is in receiving and recognising and reconciling and declaring the law. In one sense it can be said that the law is what the courts say it is; in another sense, that the courts are not their own masters, but are instruments of the law, and must reach their decisions ('findings') in accordance with law, not with the whims of judges or jurymen. Both the law and the courts, then, are rightly said to be authoritative, but in different senses, the one a silent, the other a speaking authority. To say that the authority of either is superior to the other is a misleading account of a relation far more complex than that. In the same way, the Caliph Uthman, by whose authority the standard version of the Koran was promulgated (Rahman, 1966, 40), was not thought of as the source of the Koran, but as the appropriate authority to proclaim a single version of it to all Muslims. In one sense it can be said that the Koran consists of what the Caliph declared it to consist of, in the order, still followed, in which he promulgated it. In another sense, the Caliph may be said to have been subordinate to the Koran, since his declarations were supposed to be made, not at his own whim, but in accordance with the word of God. Both Koran and Caliph, then, may be called authoritative, but in different senses, and to speak of the authority of either as superior to the other is a misleadingly simple account of a relation far more complex than that. And Islam, again like a system of law, has had the scholarly authority of its juris-consults, men learned in the law, who have had the kind of authority that goes with knowing something, not the kind of authority that goes with commanding or deciding.

Even Islam, then, has not been solely a religion of the book, with the watchword: *sola scriptura.* Rather, there have in practice been other kinds of authority beside that of the Koranic text, and it is hard to see how some form of speaking authority could be avoided in principle. An authority, institutional or personal, which promulgates a sacred text or declares it to be authoritative, is at the same time proclaiming itself to be authoritative, and exercising the authority it pro-claims. Interpretative judgements and rulings on the text are likewise pronounced with the appropriate kind of authority, scholarly or institutional. This is so even among the Sunni Muslims, the majority branch of Islam; the speaking authorities may not have been believed to be entirely inerrant, but it was thought to be necessary for Muslims to consult them or to obey them. And among the Shia Muslims, where more was claimed on behalf of the institutional authorities, it would make no sense to overlook what was believed to be the point of those authorities: they, no less than the Caliphs, were thought to have been given the care of divine revelation, but for particular purposes: to preserve it intact and to transmit it, not to do with it whatever they pleased.

There are good functional reasons, then, why speaking authorities, institutional and scholarly, are found associated with religions which are thought to be revealed. Religions without such a belief may still exhibit authority in other senses: the authority of designated functionaries to perform certain ceremonies or to make certain decisions, or the authority of learned men who know more than others know about that religion's writings or ceremonies or myths. But where it is believed that there is a divine message to be safe-guarded, more extensive authoritative roles may be thought appropriate, to resolve disputes about the content or the meaning of that message, and to pass it on without cor-ruption. W.M. Southgate has observed of sixteenth-century

England that what was at issue then in religious disputes was 'the ultimate sanction for doctrine rather than divergence over particular doctrines', so that

> In the end every man and every communion had to face the question and answer satisfactorily: not merely *what do I believe*, but *by what authority do I believe it?* (Southgate, 1962, vii)

Beliefs even in the divinely-guaranteed inerrancy of certain human pronouncements are not out of keeping with belief in a divine revelation. They would be entirely inappropriate unless it were believed that God has spoken.

8 RIGHTFUL AUTHORITY: RIGHTS TO COMMAND AND OBLIGATIONS TO OBEY

Authority may be associated with obligations: one person may be said to have a right to issue commands which others have an obligation to obey. Command and obedience, indeed, would seem to be necessarily related, in that it would be odd to speak of rightful commands which no one was obliged to obey, and in the same way the connection between obligation and authority (in the present sense of rightful authority) has been held to be analytic. Hanna Pitkin compares authority with promising:

> . . . there is no . . . answer to the question 'why does any promise ever oblige?' beyond calling attention to the meaning of the words . . . there is a *prima facie* obligation involved in each, and normally you must perform it. (Pitkin, 1966, 40, 48)

The very word *command*, indeed, is out of place unless there is some semblance of a right to issue it, and such peremptory communications as 'Your money or your life' are more properly called *demands*. Again, when someone is said to have abused or exceeded his authority, there is an implication that his authority, in the absence of such excess or abuse, was in some sense rightful. In this usage, then, the word *authority* is out of place unless it is rightful, and an expression like 'wrongful authority' can make no sense. So understood, authority (in the sphere of command at least) will always be associated with obligation.

The converse, of course, does not hold, for some cases of obligation are not associated with authority. The notion of obligations to oneself seems difficult to avoid when we think of the censure normally implied in the word *imprudence*. But the expression 'having authority over oneself' sounds odd, like the expression 'governing or commanding or obeying oneself', or 'making a promise to oneself'. (All of these expressions are used, of course, but in senses remote from the sense in which we command, govern, obey, or make promises to other people.)

Leaving aside the question of obligations to ourselves, we find that we certainly have obligations to people who have no authority over us. Indeed, we may have obligations to our subordinates. And most cases of contractual obligation do not involve authority. The parties to a contract assume obligations to one another, but they do not normally assume authority over one another. Likewise with promising: we may hold that obligations can be assumed when a promise is made — indeed, that this is what it means to make a promise — without holding that the promiser puts himself under the authority of the person to whom he makes the promise.

On the other hand, some authority has been thought to originate in a promise or a contract, and it has even been asserted that authority, at least among adults, depends logically upon the consent of those subject to it. Such approaches to authority can be most easily sustained, it would seem, in cases of membership of a voluntary association. If I have joined a club voluntarily, and can likewise resign at will, the office-bearers of the club may claim that I have subjected myself to their authority, and to the authority of the club rules, by my own consent, that as long as I remain a member my consent stands, and that if, according to the rules, they impose penalties on me for breaches of the rules, they do this by an authority which has as its sole source my own consent.

Even this claim will not be universally accepted. R.P. Wolff may be taken as a contemporary spokesman for the view that not even my own consent can create a right to my obedience, since no person can rightfully promise to obey another. Such a promise, he explains, would be potentially at variance with what he calls 'moral autonomy', which seems to consist of doing one's best to arrive at a true opinion about right and wrong with respect to each action performed, and being prepared to act on that opinion. And since the preservation of moral autonomy is what moral conduct means, it can never be right to promise to act as someone else commands, or to take that command as a reason for doing anything other than what seems to me the best thing to do at the time when I do it. (I may, with Wolff's blessing, do what someone else tells me to do, because I believe it to be the right thing to do, and not because he tells me to do it, for that would not be a case of obedience at all, and no question of authority would arise.) There can, then, be no such thing as morally rightful authority, according to Wolff; the very expression is incoherent.

Wolff's assertion that it is incompatible with the notion of moral conduct to do as someone else commands because he commands it, or to promise to do so, has been considered in Chapter 6. But his attitude to authority that it can never be rightful, even when it is consented to, can be thought of as an extension of the much more widespread notion that authority is always suspect, guilty until proven innocent. Mill may speak for multitudes: 'Each free man must think for himself and make his own choices . . . to be directed by an external authority is to sacrifice liberty.' In this line of thought, there may be a place for rightful authority, even without consent, but it is admitted grudgingly for the rearing of immature children and the government of backward peoples, where the aim must be the dismantling of authority as soon as it ceases to be necessary, and the danger, that it will be extended beyond the point of necessity. Authority has as its sole justification the deficiencies which it is the end of authority to remedy, thus bringing to an end its own justification. And among 'free men', no longer subject to the authority associated with necessary tutelage, authority will be justified only where it is consented to. Even such authority by consent is not much emphasised by Mill, who seems to believe that most good things are brought about by the independent action of individual persons, rather than by the sort of combined effort which requires some kind of authority to coordinate it (Mill, *On Liberty*).

Voluntary associations, from which members may resign at will, are not the only kind of situation in which subordination is accepted voluntarily. A seaman may sign on, voluntarily subordinating himself to shipboard authority for the duration of the voyage. A soldier, enlisting voluntarily, may subject himself to military authority for a stipulated period of time. In other cases a person may, by his own consent, subject himself to an authority which will bind him as long as he lives; the voluntary beginning of subjection in no way imples the possibility of withdrawal at will. Citizenship can be renounced in some countries, but not in all. It is true that liberal opinion has been uneasy at the thought of any subordination from which the subject cannot withdraw at will or at least after a stipulated period, even if it has been assumed voluntarily; but the example of Hobbes reminds us that it is possible to insist that the origin even of civil authority is the consent of subordinates, without imagining that this implies a right to withdraw at will.

No one could insist more strongly than Hobbes that authority can originate only in the consent of those subject to it (*Leviathan,* 21). Authority based on natural inequality cannot stand, for there is no significant natural inequality: men are approximately equal in the only respect that counts, that is, in their capacity to harm one another. Traditional authority is no better founded. By ridiculing or ignoring authority which is not founded on consent, Hobbes leaves no place for any authority other than the authority which men create for themselves, and over themselves.

To make authority the artefact of those who are subject to it, to found it on their consent, to insist that, in a world of equal men, authority is not simply in possession, but always stands in need of justification, might seem to be an approach well calculated to tame, limit and domesticate authority; but again this turns out not to be so. Authority is Leviathan, and must be so if it is to serve the purpose of those whose consent created it. If Leviathan is tamed, fettered by the need to renew its mandate and their consent, it cannot protect them from one another. And against those who might cavil at the suggestion that consent is compatible with coercion, Hobbes insists that each person's consent must extend to his own future coercion: he makes himself the author of all the sovereign's acts, not excluding acts of coercion against himself, for any more restricted consent is incompatible with the purpose of his consent, civil peace and order (*Leviathan*, 18).

When consent is offered as a *justification* of authority, it is sometimes objected that, in the case at hand, it has not been made clear what is to count as consent, or that anything properly called consent has taken place. Apparent consent may be better ascribed to coercion, deception, ignorance, immaturity, or insanity. All this is commonplace. What needs to be added is that even genuine consent is not always accepted as creating genuine rights and obligations. The parties to a criminal conspiracy may be of sound mind and mature years, well-informed, undeceived and uncoerced, without any rights or obligations issuing from their consent; we may hesitate to ascribe rightful authority to a bandit chief even when we believe that his followers have consented to obey him. *Nemo dat quod non habet:* we can give only what is ours, and likewise my consent will give rise to genuine rights and obligations, and, where appropriate, to rightful authority, only if it is clear that the matter was one in which consent was rightfully mine to give or to withhold. If banditry is a wrongful activity, bandit 'authority' can hardly be rightful authority, any more than a bandit can have a rightful claim to 'his share' of the loot. My consent to the disposal of my own possessions will be more readily accepted than my consent to the disposal of someone else's, and my consent to the disposal of my own life will make the homicide rightful only if it is beyond dispute that my life is rightfully at my disposal. The fact of consent does not make it unnecessary, still less improper, to ask questions about my right to give it, and consent creates rights and obligations only if it is rightful consent. That is why nothing is gained by attempting, as Hobbes does, to explain *all* rights and obligations in terms of consent, and authority in terms of authorisation; on the contrary, authorising and consenting can themselves be understood only in terms of a right to do so, to give consent or to authorise.

Of course the word *consent,* it seems, does not always refer to the actual consent of specific persons, but sometimes to what an imaginary person, marked sometimes by enlightened altruism and sometimes by enlightened self-interest, might be imagined to consent to, if he were asked, under imagined circumstances of complete information or, oppositely, under a veil of ignorance. Rights and obligations, including those associated with authority, may be justified along these lines, but it is a very different kind of justification, one in terms of order, justice, utility, equity, and so on, and the existence of actual consent is beside the point: such a justification of authority will neither be strengthened by the actual consent of specific persons, nor weakened by its absence (Locke, 1955, II, 119 cf. 95).

But it is not always as a *justification* of authority that

consent is offered. Harry Beran sets out to show that consent is essential to authority, not morally but as he puts it, logically, that

> there does not seem to be a single plausible case of A being in authority over B where both are sane adults and where such authority does not logically depend on B's consent. (Beran, 1978, 17)

His case is strongest when he deals with the authority of governments over naturalised adult citizens who have accepted allegiance by an act of explicit consent, though he is prepared to allow tacit consent also provided that nothing they have done can count as consenting unless something could have been done which could count as refusing to consent (Beran, 1977, 269); merely to remain within the borders of a country is no clear sign of allegiance voluntarily accepted if the borders are floodlit, patrolled and mined. And his position encounters difficulties, as he recognises, over the authority of such persons as prison governors and the commanders of conscript armies, and over parental and divine authority. The prison governor, he says, exercises authority which is delegated to him by the government, whose authority rests in its turn upon consent; but for Beran's purposes this will hardly do, for even if there is no doubt that C and D have consented to the authority of A over B, B himself has not consented to it. And parental and divine authority Beran sets aside, not entirely satisfactorily, as atypical instances of authority (Beran, 1978, 14-18), which restricts typical instances to those involving sane adults, who, he suggests, are in the relevant respects substantially equal. Beran then seems to be asserting little more than that an equal can become a subordinate only by subordinating himself, a position perhaps rather less interesting, but a good deal more plausible, than that all genuine authority logically implies the consent of its subordinates.

Moreover, Beran does not deny that power over subordinates may sometimes be morally justified in the absence of their consent. The moral justification, it appears, would need to rest on such considerations as the subordinates' needs or their inability to consent. Government without the consent of the governed may, he says, have *morally justified power,* but it has no authority, for that is not what authority means (Beran, 1977, 262-3). There seems little to be gained by this restricted use of the word authority, which denies one of its recognised meanings. And to end, as Beran does, by saying that morally justifiable power is possible in the absence of consent, would in one normal usage be taken as an assertion that *authority* is possible in the absence of consent, the contrary of what he seems to have set out to show. This part of his argument would appear to be entirely verbal.

Certainly rightful authority has not always been thought to rest on the consent of those subject to it. Parents, teachers, elders, experts, wise men, good men, men, members of particular families, and so on, have been thought to have a right to their subordinates' obedience, but the subordinates' consent has been seen as an aspect of their obligations as subordinates, not as the source of the authority over them. Each of these titles to authority has been accompanied by appropriate justifications, which have seldom included consent, and each has had its own sphere of competence and its own limits. To offer justifications of authority or to ask for them, does not become appropriate only when the authority is thought to rest on consent. And when authority is said to be in crisis, to have broken down, and so on, these expressions usually refer to forms of authority which its subordinates may recognise, but which their recognition is not thought to create, for it rests on other grounds. These grounds are various. The needs of the subordinates themselves are the usual justification of the authority of parents and teachers. The needs of other people, which can be met only by the co-ordinated efforts of bystanders in an emergency, may be held to justify the authority of the person who happens to co-ordinate them, and to give rise to an obligation on their part to submit to his direction, so that their consent is an aspect of their obligation, not the source of it, and authority, in the sense of a *right* to their compliance, exists whether they comply or not. In this sense, then, an authority cannot 'break down' or be 'in crisis' by reason of anyone's failure to accept or comply with it, for that is not where its justification lies. To write, as Alasdair MacIntyre does, of the absence 'in our society' of authority, of 'an agreed right way of doing things' (MacIntyre, 1967, 53), is to darken counsel, for there is no

necessary connection between *agreed* and *right.* There may
be a right way of doing something that there is no agreement
about at a particular time and place, unless *right* is used as
meaning *agreed,* or as implying agreement. Only if it is
accepted that consent or consensus is the sole foundation of
authority will the absence of consent or consensus deprive
authority of its justification. (To establish beyond reasonable
dispute the extent and intensity of consensus among a group
of people is, in any event, an enterprise beset by great difficulties, conceptual as well as empirical, of which those who
write about consensus do not always show themselves to be
aware.)

Some forms of authority would seem to be indispensable,
and yet can scarcely be imagined to be founded on their
subordinates' consent. Parental authority, of which almost
everyone has experience, is the clearest instance, for human
beings spend many years unable to fend for themselves, and
their rearing can only take place in a state of subordination.
It is difficult to conceive, then, on what grounds some
measure of parental authority could be denied, whatever
doubts there may be about its limits or the effectiveness of
its exercise. It is no less difficult to see it as being founded on
children's consent, and invalid in the absence of that consent.
Nor is it much more plausible to look for its foundation in
social consensus, in the consent, so to speak, of the other
adult members of the community. The absence of such consensus may indeed make more difficult the exercise of
authority by parents or guardians, but the needs of children
which arise from their protracted dependence, and which
constitute the reason for parental authority, are what they
are, whether or not they are recognised widely in this community or that. Others indeed may regulate the exercise of
parental authority, impose restrictions on it, and assume
particular parental functions, even take over the role of
parents or guardians who are unable or unwilling to exercise
it, but it is difficult to see those others, even the whole body
of them, as the source of parental authority which would not
otherwise exist, and which they delegate to those who
exercise it.

When authority is not thought to arise from the consent of
subordinates, it is often justified by reference to an inequality

of some kind between superiors and subordinates. An apprentice, we may be told, does not know his trade, and can learn it only by working under the direction of a master craftsman, whose authority comes to an end when the apprentice himself becomes a master craftsman; the end, the justification, and the limit of parental authority is the bringing of children from the dependence of infancy to the relative independence of maturity. The inferiority of subordinates to superiors will not always be found, and need not be found, in every respect, but only in those respects held to be relevant to the authority in question. The superior wit or good looks of the apprentice, the superior sensitivity or intelligence of the child, will not necessarily be thought to deprive of its justification the authority to which they are subject.

In other cases, natural inequality may be both complete and ineradicable. The rule of Prospero over Caliban is both comprehensible and just; the rule of Caliban over Prospero would be preposterous. And authority not thought to rest on consent may not be thought to rest on unequal capacity, either. When a person without official standing takes charge in an emergency, his authority will not necessarily be thought to depend upon his being the *most* competent person at giving orders, if the need is merely for some single person to direct the efforts of the rest.

And whether or not there is inequality between superiors and subordinates, to understand the justification for an authority is to understand its limits. Beyond these limits it will be proper to speak of the authority being exceeded or abused. The possibility of abuse and excess is implied by the idea of rightful authority, just as it can make sense to speak of the abuse of authority only by reference to an authority which is rightful. In the same way, though 'Property is theft' is a memorable slogan, we cannot understand rightful ownership by reference to theft, but must understand theft by reference to rightful ownership.

A rightful command must constitute a reason why it ought to be obeyed, if there is such a thing as a rightful command. In some cases it may be a reason so weighty that it would be difficult to imagine an adequate countervailing reason; in other cases it may be more easily trumped by a better reason to the contrary. Likewise, authority abused or exceeded may confer on the subject a right, or even a duty, to disregard its command, but not necessarily; in other cases there may be stronger reasons for complying with an authority even when it is being abused. Rightful authority, then, may be accorded a measure of indulgence. A subordinate, in doubt about the moral propriety of a command addressed to him, may see it as his duty to extend to a rightful authority the benefit of any such doubt.

Presumably the limit of such indulgence is reached when the subject is commanded to perform a wicked act, for it can hardly make sense to speak of a right to command wrongdoing, or of an obligation to obey such a command.

To obey a command is to accept the command as a reason for acting as commanded, indeed, as a stronger reason than one's own judgement or preference. Conversely, to follow one's own judgement or preference, to act for that reason, is not to obey an authority. Hence the attitude to authority, ranging from suspicion to hostility, among those who believe that the only rational thing to do, or that the only moral thing to do, is to act at all times on one's own judgement. (See Chapter 6.) From this point of view, to comply with authority will always be in some measure to abdicate one's own judgement, and so to be morally objectionable, or at best suspect. The obvious reply is that it is not irrational to defer to someone else's judgement if one has reason to believe that his judgement is more reliable than one's own. This may well be the case where the authority is grounded on inequality. Father *does* know best, most of the time, though Child will be less able to see this the further he is from maturity. And even when there is no such inequality, and when the person in authority is no more capable than his subordinates, it is not necessarily either irrational or morally reprehensible to act on his judgement rather than their own. Every musician in an orchestra would be capable of exercising his own judgement over when to begin playing and when to stop, and some of them may have better judgement than the conductor has; but unless he is a very bad conductor indeed, they will play better as an orchestra by acting on his judgement rather than their own. In doing so, they may continue to believe that his judgement is defective in general, or mistaken in particular. Their outward conformity to his authority is, in most cases, sufficient. They can follow his beat while neither liking him nor respecting his judgement.

It is sometimes suggested that commands are possible only with regard to outward actions, and not to feelings or beliefs. This would seem to be a mistake. It will often be difficult, and sometimes impossible, to obey a command such as 'Pull yourself together!' But then a command to perform an outward action, such as to advance in battle, may not be easy to obey, either. Again, it will often be impossible for the person in authority to tell whether a command has been obeyed if it relates to beliefs or feelings, where there is wide scope for dissimulation. But it may also be possible to pretend to obey a command to perform an action. Actions are on the whole more amenable to voluntary control than beliefs and feelings are; but it is commonly assumed that commands such as 'Stop feeling sorry for yourself' can be obeyed. To whatever degree beliefs and feelings are amenable to voluntary control, to that degree there need be nothing ridiculous in the idea of commanding them.

Authority, in the sense of a right to issue commands and a corresponding obligation on the part of someone else to obey them, may arise from the consent of a person subject to it, provided that the consent is his to give. The contention that we can never have good enough reason for deferring to someone else's judgement or obeying his commands, even with our own consent, would seem not to be well founded. Where authority in this sense rests on consent, it may be revocable, but need not be. And on the other hand the consent of subordinates seems not to be the sole origin of all rights to issue commands, for there are some such rights, notably those of parents, which it is implausible either to deny or to found upon consent, and much more plausible to found upon the subjects' needs, or upon some other basis. Whatever the reason for a right to command, to understand that reason is to understand the authority's proper limits. And though commands usually relate to outward actions, there seems to be no good reason to deny authority over whatever can be voluntarily controlled, not only over voluntary actions, but also over beliefs and feelings, to the extent to which these are under the subjects' voluntary control.

9 CIVIL AUTHORITY

Of civil or political authority, it has been asked where it lies, how it arises, and what its scope and limits are. These questions are not closely related, and need not arise together; a dispute over who are the rightful bearers of civil authority need not concern its extent, and vice versa. Likewise, agreement about an appropriate procedure for selecting an office-bearer need not imply that the procedure is the *source* of his authority. The pope is elected, but his authority is not thought to be delegated to him by those who elected him and the same attitude may be taken to a civil official who is elected: that the election is not the source of the authority of his office, but only the procedure, or part of the procedure, by which he was appointed to it. And to say that a civil office is rightly filled by primogeniture, acclamation or election is not necessarily to settle any disputes about the extent of the authority attached to it.

Notions of the origin of civil authority are sometimes classified as either descending from above by delegation or ascending from below by consent or contract. A minor official showing a written warrant, and a constitution pre-amble claiming divine warrant, are two dissimilar expressions of the former notion of civil authority, and a newly-elected politician claiming a popular mandate for his policies is the most familiar expression of the latter notion. Descending notions of the source of civil authority are sometimes thought to be associated with expansive notions of its extent; but that association would seem at best to be accidental. There is no obvious conceptual difficulty in thinking of a person's authority as being delegated from above, even from God, but very closely restricted in its extent. Likewise, the most far-reaching authority can without obvious confusion be claimed, and has been claimed, by governments which also claim to have derived it entirely from popular consent.

But there are also notions of the source of civil authority which cannot readily be called either ascending or descending.

If civil authority is claimed on behalf of those who are better educated, better organised, better born, or better able to understand the course of history, such an understanding of civil authority comes closest to the understanding of parental authority as having its source in differences, whether natural or acquired, temporary or permanent, in the capacities or abilities of human beings. Superior capacities, inherent in the bearer of authority, justify his authority; it does not come to him from any external source, either above or below him. A claim in this form may, of course, be associated with additional claims to divine or popular warrant, but not always; it some- times stands by itself. And if an additional claim to popular consent is made, that consent may be thought to add little to a claim that rests almost entirely on the superior capacities of the authority-holders.

Again, civil authority is sometimes justified by reference to the good it does or the evil it prevents, which could not other- wise be done or prevented. Of course, the evil done by governments, and the good prevented, may deprive such a justification of some of its plausibility, and lend support to the contention of philosophical anarchists that civil authority can never be justified. Such a position is usually associated with the belief that order need not depend on law, and that in the absence of civil authority there would not in fact be civil disorder, the war of all against all. On that same question of fact, non-anarchists are commonly less optimistic:

> No sooner, however, have we roughed out an anarchist charter, than we admit that a paralysis of the organs of state power or a deep dispute over the locus of political authority may be a great evil. Men so different in tempera- ment and moral outlook as Hobbes and Pascal have held that civil war is the supreme secular evil and that one ought to be prepared to pay an extraordinarily stiff price to escape it. (Cameron, in Todd, 1962, 199)

Once again, the claim that a government's authority is justified by the good it does may be, but is not always, accompanied by a claim that it has the consent of its subjects. And even if the additional claim is made, it may be added that it would not be right for subjects to withhold their consent, and that in the absence of consent the government's authority would still be adequately justified by the good it does.

To be subject to civil authority is to be affected in ways which do not necessarily involve command and obedience, for not every governmental pronouncement is a command. A decision of my government may implicate me without commanding me to do anything, as when my suburb is changed from one electoral constituency to another. But most discussion of civil authority concerns obedience to it, submission to it, compliance with it.

Civil authority may be attacked or justified at several levels: in general; in a particular form (monarchical, elective, etc.); a particular government; a particular institution or official of that government; and a particular exercise of authority. A successful attack on civil authority in general will destroy everything below it on the list, leaving every form of government, every government and every decision without justification. On the other hand, a successful attack on a particular decision as an *abuse* of authority need not implicate the authority, within its rightful limits, of the official or the government that made it. And justifications of particular decisions or policies need not amount to a justification of the authority of the government in question, or of government in general. In the same way, some justifications of government in general may give me no help in deciding whether I ought to obey a particular law, or, in time of civil strife, in deciding where my allegiance lies. I may hold that civil obligation binds me because of the civil order which government provides, but must still decide how that end is related to my obeying this or that law, or to conflicting claims on my civil allegiance.

Rightful authority in any sphere would seem to imply some kind of obligation on someone's part to obey it, and in the case of civil authority, to imply some kind of obligation on the part of those subject to it. Hart observes of promises that their breaking is an occasion for blame, but their keeping not normally an occasion for praise; for to keep a promise is to do no more than is normally expected of anyone, and the keeper of a promise is not usually praised '. . . except when marked by exceptional conscientiousness, endurance, or resistance to special temptation' (Hart, 1961, 166-7). The same observation may be made about authority, including civil authority: that once it is recognised as rightful, compliance with it is not normally praised, but taken for granted. And civil or political obligation is not in a separate category, distinct from moral obligation; if there is an obligation to obey the laws, it is a moral obligation. But not all laws command or forbid. Some laws enable, or empower, and so create no obligation to obey them. Moreover, the legal command or prohibition may not be the only reason for complying with a particular law. We may be forbidden by various laws to commit manslaughter, to maltreat children, to drive while drunk, to keep unlicensed dogs, and to park cars in certain places; and the reasons (apart from the legal prohibition) against doing these things vary greatly in their importance, some of the reasons being very much more important than the legal prohibition itself. There is, then, no single reason for obeying the law in all these matters, apart from the legal prohibition against all of them (Flathman, 1973, 107).

An authoritative command or prohibition, of course, is itself a reason for obeying it, if there is any such thing as rightful authority. And in the case of civil authority, some would go on to assert that its command is in every circumstance a sufficient reason to obey it, outweighing any other reasons to the contrary. Hobbes allows himself to be read in this way, by reiterating that the command of the sovereign cannot be unjust. But his standpoint is less crude than it appears, for he uses the word *just* in a sense so restricted that a command may be 'just', but iniquitous (*Leviathan,* 21), so that to say that the command of the sovereign is necessarily just is to make little more than a definitional point. On the other hand, Tuck speaks of those in authority, and particularly in civil authority, as sometimes having a right to do what is wrong, and Wolff defends his rejection of civil authority partly on the ground that to accept civil authority is necessarily to accept it without limits, as a 'right of the state to command the individual, and [an] obligation [for him] to obey, whatever may be commanded' (Tuck in Laslett and Runciman, 1972, 199-200; Wolff, 1970, 49). Such a claim made on behalf of civil authority would indeed be in potential conflict with moral obligation. But to save civil authority from this part of Wolff's assault, it is sufficient to deny any claim to unlimited and unconditional obedience, asserting instead that the command of a rightful authority, like a promise, gives rise to obligation *prima facie,* but that, again like a promise, it is only one source of obligations. The various obligations that bind us are not always compatible. If the obligation to keep a promise, or to obey the command of a rightful civil authority, were incompatible with the obligation to save someone's life, then presumably the third obligation would take precedence, as the weightiest of the three. But that does not mean that the other two are not genuine moral obligations; merely that neither of them is in itself an overriding moral obligation. Accordingly, just as there is no evident absurdity in saying that, *prima facie,* promises ought to be kept, but that this particular promise need not, even ought not to be kept, so there is no evident absurdity in saying of any command, including the command of a rightful civil authority, that in the face of other obligations still more serious, it ought not to be obeyed. A conscientious objector, in denying the rightfulness of his government's command to him to fight in a war that he considers iniquitous, is not necessarily impugning its authority in general, or in any other particular matter.

So we may hold that not even civil authority has a right to command wrongdoing. Its rightful sphere may be very extensive. When disputes arise about what is, morally, the right thing to do, one use of authority, and particularly of civil authority, is to settle those disputes where it is important that they be settled. If it is to do this effectively, its subjects will need to show some readiness to accept its awards, even when they consider them to be hasty, ill-advised, burdensome, or inequitable. Even when it is commanding them to act rather than to endure, civil authority may be entitled to the benefit of a subject's doubts about the moral acceptability of its commands. On the other hand, if the subject has no doubt that what he is being commanded to perform is a wicked act, there is no obvious way in which the command of the civil authority can make it right for him to obey, though it may go some distance towards excusing him.

There is, of course, some plausibility in Hobbes's sharp distinction between sovereign authority and all other authorities — *Non est potestas super terram quae comparetur ei (Job* 41:24) as the title page of the *Leviathan* says. Someone must have the last word, and the authority which draws the limits between the spheres of all other authorities, and which is not itself limited by any of them, is not in a symmetrical relationship with them: civil authority, Hobbes insists, is not an authority like any other. But while it is true that in any particular decision someone must have the last word, and that only one word can be the last, it does not seem always to be true that the last word on everything issues from the same mouth, nor that it has always been thought that this ought to be so. Governments may sometimes speak of all institutions in their territory exercising authority only by the government's command or permission; in practice, however, governments do not usually act as though they can issue any command whatever, confident of its being thought necessarily weightier than any other, and obeyed in preference to any other. Laski suggests the proscribing of the Catholic religion as an example of the kind of enactment unlikely to be passed by a British parliament, 'parliamentary sovereignty' notwithstanding (Laski, 1917, Ch. I). Nor does it seem to be true, as Hobbes suggests, that to assert limits on one's obligation to obey, necessarily amounts to a claim to replace the present sovereign, that is, simply to be sovereign (*Leviathan,* 29). In many cases there is no such claim, and all that is being asserted is that there is no authority, not even Caesar's, which rightfully has the last word on any matter whatever on which it speaks. Asserting that there are some things which are not Caesar's is not necessarily a claim to replace Caesar and to become Caesar; indeed, those who have made that assertion have often thought it important to deny explicitly that they were making any claim to civil authority.

To say this is to minimise the differences between civil authority and authority of other kinds, to regard civil authority as one authority among many, broader in its scope than most, but limited, as they all are, by the ends that each serves. But civil authority is sometimes distinguished very sharply from other forms of authority. Thus Adams asserts that, while 'all particular authority is limited as to ends . . . the objective of the polity is nothing less than that of the moral enterprise itself' (Adams, in Harris, 1976, 8). It was on that ground that unique importance was often accorded to civil authority in Greek political thought. According to Plato and

Aristotle, while particular good ends may be pursued by particular persons or groups of persons, they are restricted and incomplete unless subsumed into the common good which all of them pursue together in the *polis* (Aristotle, *Politics,* 1252a). The institutions of the *polis* may indeed be the products of human artifice and choice and agreement, but not all choices are equally appropriate, for it is also true, whether recognised or not, that man is by nature *zoon politikon,* with potentialities that will remain undeveloped unless he lives and participates in the common enterprise of the *polis.* Even the study of politics gains a reflected lustre from the universality of its subject-matter:

> Since, therefore, politics makes use of the other practical sciences, and lays it down besides what we must do and what we must not do, its end must include theirs. And that end, in politics as well as in ethics, can only be the good for man. For even if the good of the community coincides with that of the individual, the good of the community is clearly a greater and more perfect good . . . (Aristotle, *Nichomachean Ethics,* 1094b)

Rome emphasised its achievements in government rather than in politics; it provided narrower opportunities for citizens to participate in the commonwealth, but a much greater degree of peace and order over far wider tracts of space and time (Virgil, *Aeneid,* vi, 851). There, too, civil authority was thought of as something far more than one kind of authority among many.

Some traces of this broad conception of civil authority survived the disappearance of the Greek *polis* and the Roman *imperium,* and the transfer to separate institutions of functions, in particular religious functions, which had previously been consolidated. In Christendom a distinction was drawn, much more sharply than in Greek or Roman political thought or practice, between the things of Caesar and the things of God (*Matthew* 22:21), and between civil and religious institutions. It could no longer be asserted that the civil sphere comprehended all important human activities, for there was a range of important activities — indeed, the most important activities — which were not pursued in the civil sphere at all, but through the church. That institution, having established itself independently of civil governments and often in spite of them, proved able to survive the fall of most of those governments. And even within the attenuated civil sphere, some of the more exalted claims formerly made on behalf of governments were no longer plausible; no government swayed and defended the whole civilised Western world, as Rome had done, and even the provision of internal peace within narrow frontiers, and their defence against invasion, were for many governments unrealistically high aspirations. The simple and centralised picture of civil authority found in Justinian's *Institutes,* with the emperor *solus conditor legis,* survived in Byzantium, but gave place in the West to something much more complex, a network of overlapping authorities with rights and obligations which were limited by traditions, by written or unwritten laws, and by contractual agreements. There were countervailing authorities as well as countervailing powers, and civil authority came much closer to being one among several forms of authority.

It regained some of its former uniqueness towards the end of the Middle Ages, with the strengthening of centralised territorial governments that were identified by the novel word *States,* and the weakening of countervailing regional and sectional immunities and autonomies. Marsilius and many more obscure writers accorded the central place to civil authority (Skinner, 1978; Marsilius, 1951), but even Aquinas, half a century earlier and without their involvement in political controversy, was enough of an Aristotelian to depict civil authority as very much more than one among several forms of authority (Aquinas, *Summa Theologiae,* 2a 2ae, 64, 3; 1a 2ae, 90, 3). Custom came to count for less as the source of rights and obligations, including those of the prince: instead, the prince was spoken of as their source, and lesser authorities as deriving their rights and obligations from him. Roman law, then enjoying an enlarged influence, reflected and reinforced this newly simplified, pyramidal picture of civil authority. Religion retained in some measure an independent standing which it had never had in pre-Christian Greece or Rome; yet not even religious authority escaped entirely the tendency to see all existing institutions as agents or delegates of a civil government which was the source of their authority. State churches, by law established, were set up in most Protestant-ruled states, and the independence of the church was greatly reduced in most Catholic-ruled states. For each kingdom to take its religion from its sovereign, *cuius regio eius religio,* was by the mid-seventeenth century accepted in the Treaty of Westphalia as a principle on which to end an intractable war; so far had the relation between civil and religious authority altered to the detriment of the latter.

This simplification and centralisation of European governments in practice was reflected in sixteenth- and seventeenth-century political thought. With Hobbes, there is a single fount of authority, and authorities apart from the sovereign, such as the nobility, the universities, or the church, have no independent claims, but exercise only such authority as the sovereign has delegated to them. There can be no thought of the law making the king, for the law is nothing but the will of the sovereign. Even divine revelation is what the sovereign says it is: 'It is the Civil Sovereign, that is to appoint Judges, and Interpreters of the . . . Scriptures; for he it is that maketh them Laws' (*Leviathan,* 42).

And as all lesser authorities are authorised by a single authority, so that authority itself, the sovereign, arises from a single act of authorisation in which all take part; that is the sovereign's sole claim to civil authority. Hobbes speaks of 'the throne of their lawful Prince . . . whom they had themselves placed there' (*Leviathan,* 44). Instead of explaining authorisation by reference to authority, a sustained attempt is made to explain all authority by reference to authorisation, which is, as Peters observes (in Quinton, 1967, 85), 'one of its derivatives'. This reversal is the source of some of the difficulties which Hobbes's argument encounters. For it is always to the point to take the argument back one step, and ask by what authority a person claims to authorise, and what kinds of thing he may properly authorise. Hobbes's reply is not entirely satisfactory. He sometimes speaks of the sovereign's right to punish as being the sole survival of the right that every man would have in a state of nature to hurt or kill for his own preservation, 'for the subjects did not give the sovereign that right, but in laying down theirs, strengthened him to use his own'; an argument which is unnecessary if, as

Hobbes repeatedly asserts, each criminal has authorised in advance his own punishment (*Leviathan*, 28; cf. 21). Again, it is hard to see how the rights of governments to coerce and punish can be traced to any similar rights in a state of nature, since it is not obvious that private persons in a state of nature could have anything more than a right to defend themselves by force at the time and place of an unjustified attack and, perhaps, something analogous to the right of hot pursuit in international law. Civil authority does far more than that: it 'investigates past actions, tries and punishes people, and forces rules on them' (Anscombe, 1978, 18). Moreover, in more familiar cases of authorisation, though an agent may bind the person who authorises him, he has no authority over him, but rather the reverse: the principal has authority over his agent, not the agent over his principal.

Where Hobbes attempted to show that all governments necessarily possessed that consent which was the source of their authority, Locke sought to show that only some governments possessed such rightful authority, while others did not. Thus his argument runs into difficulties quite different from Hobbes's; for if Locke's requirements for consent are understood in a strong sense, we may conclude that no government has rightful authority, and if they are understood in a weak sense, we may conclude that no government lacks rightful authority. To complicate matters still further, Locke seems sometimes to be speaking about whether a government in fact has its subjects' consent, express or tacit, and sometimes about whether it is worthy of their consent, whether it is the kind of government to which an imaginary man in an imaginary state of nature might be expected to consent (Locke, 1955, II, 95, cf. 116, 119; Pitkin, 1966, 40). In the latter case, the justification offered is by merit, in the form of services provided, not by consent.

Of course, what looks like the giving of individual consent may be a purely procedural device, to designate an office-bearer, change a rule, make a decision, and so on. Such a procedure might be required, and invariably followed in situations of the appropriate type; but unless it were also thought of as the foundation or the re-foundation of the government and the renewal of its delegated authority, the question of consent being the source of civil authority need not arise at all.

Hobbes and Locke were not the only writers in their time to make use of notions of consent in their accounts of civil authority, and the prevalence of ideas that are sometimes lumped together as 'the consent theory of political obligation' has not passed unnoticed. But what was novel about seventeenth-century writing on consent is perhaps less obvious. Consent-giving procedures in civil government were no novelty in medieval Europe, and it was not unknown for coronation oaths to assert that the crown was conferred on the king by his equals (Laird, 1934, 100). And religious justifications of civil authority, which are sometimes said to have grown weaker after the Reformation, had by no means disappeared: Locke did not instantly replace Filmer. But in times of civil strife, the appeal to divine authorisation could not by itself settle disputes about which of several claimants had that authorisation. An appeal to established practices could not be conclusive, either, for some established practices in government were themselves in dispute, and others had long since been destroyed, often by governments. Change in forms of government and religious institutions emphasised that both were variable, the products of human will and artifice, and amenable to further variation. Aristotle was stood on his head; it was now the choosing individual, his judgement, his purpose, his consent, which were to be considered first, and institutions assessed as more or less useful to his purposes. An Athenian was not the product of the laws of Athens (Plato, *Crito,* 50-1), but vice versa. In these circumstances, many difficulties could be avoided if civil obligation could be shown to be self-imposed, and civil authority the creature of its own subjects.

In a few instances this required no great ingenuity. The new government in Massachusetts in 1620 was created by a written compact with signatures at the foot, made by men who were already accustomed to setting up church congregations in the same way by the voluntary adherence of members. But most states were older than any of their subjects, and it would be no straightforward task to show that the relationship of those subjects with their governments was similar in all important respects to that of signatories to the Mayflower Compact. After all, the Mayflower signatories had not merely acquiesced; they had made explicit promises, and thereby assumed civil obligations which had whatever binding force promises have. Subjects of established states had done nothing so explicit: they were not parties to a contract recorded on paper, and indeed there was usually no such contract, so that if they were said to have consented, their consent would need to be qualified by some such adjective as *tacit* or *implied.* The evidence offered for this tacit consent was something done, or not done, which was not explicitly an act of consenting at all: inheriting property, refraining from leaving the country, and so on (Locke, 1955, II, 116, 119). And it is always possible to ask whether such an act or omission is sufficient evidence for the consent which has been inferred from it.

It is always possible to ask, also, what it is that a person has tacitly consented to. An oath of allegiance or an actual civil compact could be drawn up in great detail so as to settle most disputes about what its adherents had promised to do or to refrain from. In particular, it would be possible to make clear whether they had promised

1. to refrain from armed revolt against the government;
2. to refrain from attempts to subvert the government;
3. to obey the government's commands even when it was disadvantageous to the subject to do so (for instance, to pay a heavy and inequitable tax);
4. to obey the government's commands even when they required him to perform a wicked act (for instance, to murder a prisoner-of-war).

Likewise, it would be possible in an actual civil compact to exempt certain matters from the government's authority and from the subects' obligation to obey. Tacit consent, by contrast, is undiscriminating. As there is no explicit text of the terms of agreement to refer to, it becomes more plausible to assert that civil authority and the obedience promised to it have no limits, or that there is no way of deciding what the limits are. Thus, more extensive consent to more extensive civil authority may be inferred from evidence less conclusive than would be available if there were an actual civil compact.

An explicit individual promise to obey a civil authority may be thought to be irrevocable, or revocable. If it is thought to be irrevocable, then I may still be bound by my own past consent, even if I regret having given it. And if I do not do as I promised, then I am neglecting my civil obligations, and if the civil compact is appropriately worded, I may have authorised the coercion which is exercised to enforce my compliance. If, on the other hand, my consent is thought to be revocable at will, then to withdraw my consent is to end my obligations. I can never be mistaken about my obligations, and there can be no such thing as failure to discharge them. Coercion exercised to hold me to my civil obligations can never be justified by this notion of consent. In other words, individual consent, if revocable at will, cannot be the source of civil authority and obligation at all, properly speaking. Such consent could give rise to no civil obligations, any more than marital consent similarly understood could give rise to marital obligations. Obligations bind: that is what the word means. And civil obligations over which each person has an overriding veto at any time are not obligations at all. This explains the familiar untidiness of consent theories of civil authority. They are littered with criteria of consent and constraints on consent, with notions of tacit consent, vicarious consent, majority rule, and so on, which form no part of the idea of explicit individual consent, but are indispensable if a consent theory is to provide what it cannot provide by itself: binding obligations to a civil authority.

A person may bind himself by a civil compact that he agrees to; but it is difficult to see that others who are not parties to the compact are bound in the same way. Even in Massachusetts, not every resident signed the Mayflower Compact, and yet the government's authority was not thought to be limited to signatories. If, then, it extended to non-signatories, then they had become subject to its authority without their consent; so that explicit individual consent could not have been seen as a necessary condition of all rightful civil authority. After a few years no citizen of Massachusetts would still have been alive who had explicitly given his consent to the authority of the government, so that, if its authority was still said to depend on consent, it would be their fathers' consent, not their own: a very different matter.

Explicit individual consent may be given contrary to the consenter's interest, or his duty, or both. I may enter into a disadvantageous contract, or a criminal conspiracy, in circumstances where it is not possible to impugn the genuineness of my consent, whatever questions may arise about its binding force. But in consent theories of civil authority, consent is often bolstered by interest or right. If the government governs in my interest, or (what is not necessarily the same thing) in the general interest, I may be told it does not matter much what form my consent took, or how long ago I gave it, or (according to Hume) whether I consented at all (Hume, 1965, 255-73). In this way utilitarian considerations, individual and social, may be made either to replace or to reinforce considerations of consent. There is, indeed, no necessary connection between what a Rational Man might be expected to consent to, when moved entirely by enlightened self-interest or by enlightened altruism, and what actual men consent to in fact; but the belief that they will nearly always coincide in practice may open the prospect of a society just and harmonious, with little or no coercion. Self-love and social will be the same, or nearly so, and Publick Benefits will not be seen as the outcome of Private Vices, for the pursuit of one's own advantage can hardly be seen as vicious (Bernard Mandeville, *The Fable of the Bees;* even Alexander Pope, *Essay on Man*). Obligations will be voluntarily assumed, for it will be in everyone's interest to assume them, and any residual conflict will usually be the outcome of misunderstanding. Such coercion as is still necessary will be exercised mainly over people who cannot discern where their own interests lie. Individual persons and groups will seek their advantage as they see it; indeed government itself may be seen as no more than one of these groups, and public policy as the sum of their pressures (Bentley, 1935).

Such a model for a possible society is no longer as fashionable as it once was, and the most fashionable complaint against it is that it wrongly assumes that everyone participates on equal terms, so that participation provides all the safeguards that a participant needs. But even apart from this objection, the model has serious deficiencies. It can hardly find a place for heroic individual sacrifice in the community's interest in which the individual risks death or serious injury. In every community such sacrifices are made, and in every community there are men — firemen, policemen, soldiers — whose employment involves them in taking additional risks. Yet it can hardly be said that to lay down my life for anyone else is in my own interest, unless I and my interests survive the grave. In this world it is far from obvious that everyone's interests are compatible with everyone else's. As for wants, it requires great faith to believe, with Fromm, that the world is so constituted that everyone may without conflict do as he pleases (Fromm, 1949). Weaker brethren may be invited to believe that 'Do as you please, as long as everyone else can do the same' is a workable rule for uncoerced men. But the latter version is only an apparent improvement on the former, for it provides no authoritative rule for resolving conflicts which may arise, and no means of resolving them apart from voluntary renunciation, which none of the conflicting parties can regard as doing as he pleases.

Individual consent, then, seems sometimes to be thought of as a justification of civil authority, and sometimes as an attempt to show that civil authority is unnecessary wholly or in part. The consent stipulated is sometimes explicit, and sometimes implied, sometimes narrow in its scope and sometimes broad, sometimes revocable and sometimes not. But the common strand is the contention that obedience to civil authority can be shown in some way to be merely the honouring of an undertaking that I have already given. This is sometimes confused with, but ought to be distinguished from, the notion of Rousseau and others that the commands of a civil authority that is rightly constituted are in some way the pronouncements of the considered moral judgements of each citizen. Hobbes tells us that the subjects of every government obey an authority which they have imposed on themselves, but which is distinct from themselves; Rousseau tells us that each citizen of a just government would obey only himself. There could never be conflict between the command of such a government and the moral duty of one of its citizens, for the government's voice is his own. Indeed, he can scarcely be said to obey such a government, except in the sense of 'obeying his own conscience', which is what obedience to a government like that would amount to: the authoritative voice speaks from inside him as well as from outside (Rousseau, *Social Contract* I, vi-vii and II, iii). Here, clearly, is an authority unlike any other.

But it does not seem that any actual government, or even any possible government, could fill such a demanding role. A state, or a community, does not seem to be a moral agent: it cannot be malicious or benevolent or negligent or temperate or repentant, as individual persons (including individual public officials) can. Nor can individual persons be imagined to cease to be moral agents in becoming constituent members of a body politic. Nor, if there were more than one such body politic, each the voice of the moral judgement of its citizens, is it clear how conflict between communities could be understood if it occurred.

These difficulties, and in particular the last mentioned, arise also from a reflection on classical political thought, which Rousseau was attempting in part to revive. Donelan (1978) has reminded us of the restricted views, small size and constant quarrels of the governments whose political philosophers were Plato and Aristotle. That philosophy inhabited a moral universe that was, in some respects, without limits, and was certainly not limited by the bounds of a single *polis*. It held that morals and politics, moral life and political life, are very closely related, and impossible entirely to separate. And yet its political perspective was not the world, nor the civilised world, nor the Mediterranean world, nor even the Greek world: it was the individual *polis*.

Rousseau praised the ancients, as Machiavelli had done, for offering men a single authority as a single focus for their loyalties, and in particular for avoiding the difficulties that arise from the attempt to distinguish Caesar's things from God's; but that approach had difficulties of its own. Rousseau agreed with Plato and Aristotle that good government is possible only on a very small scale, but the most extensive government, even a world state, would seem to be equally unfitted for the role that Rousseau envisages, that of issuing commands which *could not* be in conflict with a citizen's moral obligations. Certainly it could have no conflicts with other states if there were none, but internal conflicts could still be conceived of. It is not obvious that any considerations of extent, or of the absence of other states, could make it nonsensical for one of its citizens to ask whether a command of such a state was morally binding. To obey its commands could never constitute the whole duty of man, nor would disobedience be necessarily wrong. It is only in the realm of definitions that government, whether over a small community or over the whole planet, speaks in such constant harmony with the moral duty of each of its citizens that limits to civil obligation are not merely unnecessary, but undesirable. In the sublunary world, civil authority, on whatever scale, is best thought of as no more than one kind of rightful authority, the source of moral obligations *prima facie,* which need not, however, be seen as always overriding all obligations which arise in other ways.

CONCLUSION

Authority, in all its forms, is found only where a number of people are gathered together in some activity which depends upon their several roles. No one can be an authority to himself, or in authority over himself. The sphere of authority is public, not private, social, not individual. That is why it is at odds with egalitarian assumptions and notions, which are individualistic: they ask us to imagine mankind as a myriad of monads, with no parents, no infancy, no childhood, no past, none of whom was ever an apprentice, a student, a recruit, or a member of a team. But human beings as we know them are social and interdependent beings. They begin their lives in a state of the most complete dependency, and such independence as they exhibit in maturity is achieved, and effectively enjoyed, through association with other people in common activities and institutions, marked, in many cases, by authority in one or more of the senses considered above. It is by reference to some activity that every instance of authority may be understood, and, where justification is needed, justified. The limits of any authority are likewise understood by reference to the activity within which it operates. In one context the appropriate authority is a dictionary; in another, an atlas. If the instructions of parents or of firemen ought to be obeyed, it is in matters to do with child-rearing or putting out fires, and for reasons having to do with the importance of those activities. Reasons of some kind are associated with authority of every kind, though they may not always be good reasons. To obey a command, we must have some reason for doing so, and this is true even when we turn out to have been obeying an impostor. To consult a dictionary, we must believe it to be an authoritative work of reference, and this is so even if we are mistaken, and the dictionary we are consulting is an inaccurate one. And because every human activity has limits of some kind, every instance of human authority has corresponding limits; the notion of such authority being unlimited would seem to be incoherent.

But though we could not understand or recognise an authority for which there was no kind of reason, we do not expect to see these reasons recapitulated at length on every occasion when the authority is consulted, deferred to, followed, or obeyed. Indeed, it is a more typical instance of compliance with authority to stop because a policeman has put up a traffic sign than to stop because he has explained exhaustively the plan for diverting the traffic, and in some cases authority cannot function once there has been a complete explanation of the matter in hand: a person who understands a pronouncement completely, with all the reasons for it, can no longer accept it on authority (though he may still accept it), and Dr Johnson's dictionary cannot be consulted as an authority by Dr Johnson.

If authority did not normally have some justification, it would not be possible to speak of it being exceeded or abused. Justification is usually by reference to the importance (at least to the participants) of the activity with which the authority is associated, and to the importance of the authority if the activity is to be carried on. It is important for a child to learn his first language, and if he is to do so, indispensable that he should take people around him as authorities on that language. So with the various kinds of authority associated with such activities as child-rearing, scholarship, or government, or with such institutions as laboratories, universities, hospitals, or orchestras: if the activity or the institution is important, and if some kind of authority is required to carry it on, then *prima facie* that authority has all the justification that it needs. Some rough notion of its limits, too, is a part of such an understanding of any form of authority in the context of the activity or institution where it is found.

But there is an element of arbitrariness, also, in any arrangement of roles and offices. It is nearly always arguable that a different set of arrangements would enable an activity to be more effectively conducted, or an institution to function better; only rarely does it seem that the existing set of arrangements is the only one conceivable. This element of arbitrariness extends to nearly every form of authority. Alternative procedures for commanding or pronouncing, for obeying or consulting, are nearly always thinkable. And yet, if very much attention is given to these alternative possibilities, to alternative roles and offices and authorities, any activity or institution will be disrupted. Participants do not have infinite time, attention and energy, and to divert these into the search for alternative procedures is to reduce, at least in the short term, the effectiveness of what is being done. (There are, of course, situations where this disruption is a price which has to be paid.) It is impossible in principle to consider every available alternative and to describe exhaustively the advantages and disadvantages of all of them; impossible, then, to be sure that any particular alternative is the best possible one, and so the restless search for something better could delay or disrupt indefinitely the work of the institution or the pursuit of the activity. The best would be the enemy of the good, and nothing would ever be accomplished:

> And still be doing, never done:
> As if Religion were intended
> For nothing else but to be mended.   (Butler, *Hudibras,* i)

In practice, the pursuit of any activity is possible only among those who are not paralysed in the face of an endless range of alternatives, but are prepared to follow one procedure, one set of roles, one arrangement of offices, and the authority that goes with it. It is in this sense that even the most reasonable instance of authority is arbitrary; but such arbitrariness need not detract from its reasonableness. In the same way, the arbitrariness of the choice of red as the colour for stop lights does not show that it is unreasonable to stop at red lights.

Even an authority which is justified may, however, be abused, or used inappropriately. An official may exceed his commission. A learned man may make pronouncements beyond his sphere of competence. Counsel may shade into command. An authoritative work of reference may be inaccurate in some particular, and even if it is not, may mislead a person who consults it inexpertly. In these and many other ways an authority may hinder the pursuit of the very objectives on which its justification rests.

It is appropriate, then, constantly to refer every authority back to the objectives by reference to which it is recognised and understood and justified. But it is not appropriate to rail indiscriminately against authority, to yearn for its disappearance or even for its waning, to overlook its variety and its ubiquity, its indispensability to so many human activities which are themselves indispensable. Every kind of human relationship is prone to imperfection, and authoritative relationships are no exception. But without authority, in the diverse senses considered in this book, no community of human beings as we know them can be imagined.

BIBLIOGRAPHY

Acton, H.B. (ed.) (1969) *Philosophy of Punishment,* London: Macmillan

Acton, J.E.E.D. (1955) *Essays on Freedom and Power,* Clevland: World Publishing Company

Adams, P., Schwab, J. and Aponte, J. (1962) 'Authoritarian Parents and Disturbed Children', American Journal of Psychiatry, 121

Adorno, T.W. (and others) (1950) *The Authoritarian Personality,* New York: Harper & Row

Amis, K. (1954) *Lucky Jim,* London: Gollancz

Anscombe, G.E.M. (1962) 'Authority in morals', in Todd, J.M. (ed.), *Problems in Authority,* Baltimore: Helicon

—— (1978) 'On the Source of the Authority of the State', *Ratio,* 20

Arendt, H. (1954) 'What is Authority?', in *Between Past and Future: Six Exercises in Political Thought,* New York: Viking Press

—— (1956) 'Authority in the Twentieth Century', *Review of Politics,* 18

Austin, J. (1954) *The Province of Jurisprudence Determined,* New York: Noonday Press

Axinn, S. (1971) 'Kant, Authority, and the French Revolution', *Journal of the History of Ideas,* 32

Bagehot, Walter (1966) *The English Constitution,* London: Fontana

Baier, Kurt (1965) *The Moral Point of View,* New York: Cornell UP

—— (1972) 'The Justification of Governmental Authority', *Journal of Philosophy,* 69

Bantock, G.H. (1965) *Freedom and Authority in Education: A Criticism of Modern Cultural and Educational Assumptions,* 2nd edn., London: Faber & Faber

Barker, E.N. (1963) 'Authoritarianism of the Political Right, Center, and Left', *Journal of Social Issues,* 19, 63

Barnard, F.M. (1971) '"The Practical Philosophy" of Christian

Thomasius', *Journal of the History of Ideas,* 32

Bass, B.M. (1955) 'Authoritarianism or Acquiescence?', *Journal of Abnormal and Social Psychology,* 15

Bates, S. (1972) 'Authority and Autonomy', *Journal of Philosophy,* 69

Bays, D.H. (1970) 'The Nature of Provincial Political Authority in Late Ch'ing Times: Chang Chih-tung in Canton, 1884-1889', *Modern Asian Studies,* 4

Bell, D.R. (1971) 'Authority' in *The Proper Study: Royal Institute of Philosophy Lectures, 1969-1970,* London: Macmillan

Bell, D.V. (1975) *Power, Influence and Authority,* London: OUP

Benn, S.I. (1967) 'Authority', in *The Encyclopedia of Philosophy,* I, New York: Macmillan

—— and Peters, R.S. (1959) *Social Principles and the Democratic State,* London: Allen & Unwin

Benne, K.D. (1970) 'Authority in Education', *Harvard Educational Review,* 40

Bennis, W.G., Berkowitz, N. *et al.* (1958) 'Authority, Power and the Ability to Influence', *Human Relations,* 11

Bentley, Arthur (1935) *The Process of Government,* 2nd edn., Evanston: Principia

Beran, H. (1977) 'In defence of the consent theory of political obligation and authority', *Ethics,* 87

—— (1978) 'Political Authority and Consent', *Australasian Political Studies Association 20th Conference Papers,* Adelaide

Berdyaev, N. (1952) 'Man and Caesar — Authority', Ch. 4 of *The Realm of Spirit and the Realm of Caesar,* London: Gollancz

Berger, M., Abel, T. and Page, C.H. (eds.) (1954) *Freedom and Control in Modern Society,* New York: Van Nostrand

Bernard, C. (1961) 'The Theory of Authority', in *Theories of Society,* T. Parsons *et al.* (eds.), New York: Free Press

Bertocci, P. (1936) 'The Authority of Ethical Ideals', *Journal of Philosophy,* 33

Blau, P.M. (1963) 'Critical Remarks on Weber's Theory of Authority', *American Political Science Review,* 57

Bochenski, J.M. (1965) 'Analysis of Authority', in *The Logic of Religion,* New York: NYU Press

Bowe, G. (1955) *The Origin of Political Authority,* Dublin: Clonmore & Reynolds

Brandis, R. (1967) 'On the Noxious Influence of Authority', *Quarterly Review of Economics and Business,* 7

Braybrooke, D. (1960) 'Authority as a Subject of Social Science and Philosophy', *Review of Metaphysics,* 13

Bronson, W.C., Katten, E.S. and Livson, N. (1959) 'Patterns of Authority and Affection in Two Generations', *Journal of Abnormal and Social Psychology,* 58

Brown, R.W. (1953) 'A Determinant of the Relationship between Rigidity and Authoritarianism', *Journal of Abnormal and Social Psychology,* 48

Bryne, D. (1965) 'Parental Antecedents of Authoritarianism', *Journal of Personality and Social Psychology,* I

Buehrig, E.H. (1965) 'International Pattern of Authority', *World Politics,* 17

Burrill, D.R. (1966) 'Changing Status of Moral Authority', *Harvard Theological Review,* 59

Burwen, L.S. and Campbell, D.R. (1957) 'The Generality of Attitudes towards Authority and Non-authority Figures', *Journal of Abnormal and Social Psychology,* 54

Canaday, N. (1968) *Melville and Authority,* Gainesville: University of Florida Press

Carroll, J.D. (1969) 'Noetic Authority', *Public Administration Review,* 29

Carter, A. (1979) *Authority and Democracy,* Oxford: Blackwell

Cassinelli C.W. (1961) 'Political Authority: Its Exercise and Possession', *Western Political Quarterly,* 14

Catlin, G.A. (1930) *Study of the Principles of Politics, being an Essay Toward Political Rationalisation,* New York: Macmillan

Christie, R. and Cook, P. (1958) 'A Guide to Published Literature Relating to the Authoritarian Personality through 1956', *Journal of Psychology,* 45

—— and Jahoda, M. (eds.) (1954) *Studies in the Scope and Method of 'The Authoritarian Personality',* Glencoe: Free Press

Cochran, C.E. (1977) 'Authority and community', *American Political Science Review,* 71

Cohen, C. (1972) 'Autonomy and Government', *Journal of Philosophy,* 69

Collier, K.G. (1957) 'Authority, Society and Education, *Journal of Educational Sociology*, 30

Comfort, A. (1950) *Authority and Delinquency in the Modern State*, London: Routledge

Cowling, Maurice (1963) *Mill and Liberalism*, Cambridge: CUP

Cragg, G.R. (1964) *Reason and Authority in the Eighteenth Century*, Cambridge: CUP

Dahl, R.A. (1970) *After the Revolution? Authority in a Good Society*, New Haven: Yale UP

Dalton, G.W., Barnes, L.B. and Zaleznik, A. (1968) *The Distribution of Authority in Formal Organisations*, Boston: Harvard Business School

Davies, R.E. (1946) *The Problem of Authority in the Continental Reformers*, London: Epworth

Davies, W.W. (1935) 'By What Authority?' *Hibbert Journal*, 34

Day, J. (1963) 'Authority', *Political Studies*, 11

de Grazia, S. (1959) 'What Authority is *not*', *American Political Science Review*, 53

Dickinson, J. (1929) 'Social Order and Political Authority', *American Political Review*, 23

Dobriner, W.M. (1977) 'Freedom and Authority', *Yale Review*, 66

Dominian, J. (1976) *Authority*, London: Burns & Oates

Donelan, Michael (1978) *The Reason of States*, London: Allen & Unwin

Duncan-Jones, A. (1958) 'Authority', *Proceedings of the Aristotelian Society*, supplementary volume 32

Dworkin, G. (1972) 'Reasons and Authority', *Journal of Philosophy*, 69

Edgerton, S.G. (1969) 'Have we Really Talked Enough about "Authority"?', *Studies in Philosophy and Education*, 6

Encel, S. (1970) *Equality and Authority: A Study of Class, Status and Power in Australia*, London: Tavistock

Engels, F. (1972) 'On Authority', in R.C. Tucker (ed.), *The Marx-Engels Reader*, New York: Norton

Eysenck, H.J. and Wilson, G.D. (1978) *The Psychological Basis of Ideology*, Lancaster: MTP

Flathman, R.E. (1973) *Political Obligation*, London: Croom Helm

—— (1980) *The Practice of Political Authority*, Chicago: Chicago UP

Fox, W.S. *et al.* (1977) 'Authority position, legitimacy of authority structure, and acquiescence to authority', *Social Forces,* 55

Frankel, C. (1972) 'Political Disobedience and the Denial of Political Authority', *Social Theory and Practice,* 2

Freedman, M., Webster, H. and Sanford, N. (1965) 'A Study of Authoritarianism and Psychopathology', *Journal of Psychology,* 41

Freidson, E. (1968) 'The Impurity of Professional Authority', in *Institutions and the Person,* H. Becker *et al.* (eds.), Chicago: Aldine

Friedman, R.B. (1968) 'An Introduction to Mill's Theory of Authority', in J.B. Schneewind (ed.), *Mill: A Collection of Critical Essays,* London: Macmillan

—— (1973) 'On the concept of authority in political philosophy', in R.E. Flathman (ed.), *Concepts in Social and Political Philosophy,* New York: Macmillan

Friedrich, C.J. (1963) *Man and His Government,* New York: McGraw-Hill

—— (1963) 'Political Authority and Reasoning', in *Man and His Government,* New York: McGraw Hill

—— (1967) 'Power and Authority', in *An Introduction to Political Theory,* New York: Harper & Row

Fromm, Erich (1949) *Man for Himself,* London: Routledge

Gierke, O. Von (1900) *Political Theories of the Middles Ages,* Cambridge: CUP

Golightly, C.L. (1972) 'Ethics and Moral Activism', *Monist,* 56

Gouldner, A.W. (ed.) (1965) *Studies in Leadership,* New York: Russell

Greenstein, F. (1960) 'The Benevolent Leader: Children's Images of Political Authority', *American Political Science Review,* 54

Gregory, W.E. (1957) 'The Orthodoxy of the Authoritarian Personality', *Journal of Social Psychology,* 45

Grusky, O. (1962) 'Authoritarianism and Effective Indoctrination: A Case Study', *Administrative Science Quarterly,* 7

Guillaume, Alfred (1975) *Islam,* London: Penguin

Hallowell, J.H. (1954) *The Moral Foundation of Democracy,* Chicago: University of Chicago Press

Handcock, W.D. (1953) 'The Function and Nature of Authority in Society', *Philosophy,* 28

Harris, E. (1966) 'Sovereign Authority and Power', in *Annihilation and Utopia: The Principles of International Politics*, London: Allen & Unwin

Harris, R.B. (ed.) (1976) *Authority: A Philosophical Analysis*, University of Alabama Press

Harrison, P. (1959) *Authority in the Free Church Tradition*, Princeton: Princeton University Press

—— (1960) 'Weber's Categories of Authority and Voluntary Associations', *American Sociological Review*, 25

Hart, H.L.A. (1961) *The Concept of Law*, Oxford: Clarendon

Hartmann, H. (1959) *Authority and Organisation in German Management*, Princeton: Princeton University Press

Heasman, D.J. (1976) 'Liberty, authority and democracy', *Contemporary Review*, 228

Heinze, R. (1925) 'Auctoritas', *Hermes*, 9

Helm, C. and Morelli, M. (1979) 'Stanley Milgram and the obedience experiment', *Political Theory*, 7

Hess, R.D. (1963) 'The Socialisation of Attitudes Toward Political Authority: Some Cross-national Comparisons', *International Social Science Journal*, 15

Hitchcock, J. (1970) 'The State of Authority in the Church', *Cross Currents*, 20

Hopkins, T.K. (1961) 'Bureaucratic Authority: The Convergence of Weber and Barnard', in Amitai Etzioni (ed.), *Complex Organisations*, New York: Holt Rinehart

Hughes, Gerard (1978) *Authority in Morals*, London: Heythrop

Hume, David (1953) 'Of the First Principles of Government' in Frederick Watkins, *Hume's Political Essays*, New York: Bobbs Merrill

—— (1965) 'Of the Original Contract', *Hume's Ethical Writings*, New York: Collier

Huntington, S.P. and Moore, C.H. (eds.) (1970) *Authoritarian Politics in Modern Society: The Dynamics of Established One-party Systems*, New York: Basic Books

Jackson, F. (1967) 'A Note on Incorrigibility and Authority', *Australasian Journal of Philosophy*, 45

Janowitz, M. (1959) 'Changing Patterns of Organisational Authority: the Military Establishment', *Administrative Science Quarterly*, 3

—— and Marvick, D. (1953) 'Authoritarianism and Political Behavior', *Public Opinion Quarterly*, 17

Jensen, A.R. (1957) 'Authoritarian Attitudes and Personality Maladjustment', *Journal of Abnormal and Social Psychology*, 54

Jerrold, D. (1932) 'Authority, Mind and Power', *The Criterion*, 12

Johnson, C. (1971) 'The Changing Nature and Locus of Authority in Communist China', in J. Lindbeck (ed.), *China: Management of a Revolutionary Society*, Seattle: University of Washington Press

Johnson, R.C. (1959) *Authority in Protestant Theology*, Philadelphia: Westminster Press

Jouvenel, B. de (1949) *On Power, Its Nature and the History of Its Growth*, trans. J.F. Huntington, New York: Viking
—— (1957) *Sovereignty: An Inquiry into the Political Good*, trans. J.F. Huntington, Chicago: University of Chicago Press
—— (1963) *Pure Theory of Politics*, Cambridge: CUP

Kariel, H.S. (1964) *In Search of Authority: Twentieth-Century Political Thought*, New York: Free Press

Kelsen, Hans (1945) *General Theory of Law and the State*, New York: Russell

Kierkegaard, S. (1955) *On Authority and Revelation*, Princeton: Princeton University Press

Kim, Y.C. (1966) 'Authority: Some Conceptual and Empirical Notes', *Western Political Quarterly*, 19

King, Preston (1967) *Fear of Power: an Analysis of Anti-statism in Three French Writers*, London: Cass
—— (1974) *The Ideology of Order. A Comparative Analysis of Jean Bodin and Thomas Hobbes*, London: Allen & Unwin

Koestler, A. (1967) *The Ghost in the Machine*, London: Hutchinson

Krieger, L. (1973) 'Authority', in Wiener, P. (ed.), *Dictionary of the History of Ideas*, New York: Scribners
—— (1977) 'The Idea of authority in the West', *American Historical Review*, 82

Kropotkin, P. (1886) *Law and Authority*, London: International

Ladenson, R.F. (1972) 'Legitimate Authority', *American Philosophical Quarterly*, 9

Laird, J. (1934) 'The Conception of Authority', *Proceedings of the Aristotelian Society*, 34

Lasch, C. (1977) *Haven in a Heartless World: the Family Besieged*, New York: Basic Books

Lash, Nicholas (1976) *Voices of Authority*, Shepherdstown: Patmos

Laski, H.J. (1917) *Studies in the Problem of Sovereignty*, New Haven: Yale UP

—— (1919) *Authority in the Modern State*, New Haven: Yale UP

Laslett, Peter (ed.) (1956) *Philosophy, Politics and Society*, first series, Oxford, Blackwell

—— and Runciman, W.G. (eds.) (1972) *Philosophy, Politics and Society*, fourth series, Oxford: Blackwell

Leavitt, H.J., Hax, H. and Roche, J.H. (1955) '"Authoritarianism" and agreement with things authoritative', *Journal of Psychology*, 40

Leventhal, H., Jacobs, R. and Kudirka, H. (1964) 'Authoritatianism, Ideology and Political Candidate Choice', *Journal of Abnormal and Social Psychology*, 69

Lipset, S.M. (1959) 'Democracy and Working Class Authoritarianism', *American Sociological Review*, 24

Lipsitz, L. (1965) 'Working Class Authoritarianism: A Reevaluation', *American Sociological Review*, 30

Lloyd-Jones, D.M. (1958) *Authority*, Chicago: Inter-varsity

Locke, John (1955) *Two Treatises of Civil Government*, London: Dent

—— (1961) *Essay Concerning Human Understanding*, London: Dent

Lowi, T.J. (1969) *The End of Liberalism*, New York: Norton

Lukes, Steven (1974) *Power: a Radical View*, London: Macmillan

MacDonald, A.J.M. (1933) *Authority and Reason in the Early Middle Ages*, London: OUP

MacIntyre, Alasdair (1967) *Secularization and Moral Change*, London: OUP

McKenzie, J. (1966) *Authority in the Church*, New York: Sheed and Ward

MacKenzie, W.J.M. (1975) *Power, Violence, Decision*, Harmondsworth: Penguin

Mackey, J.P. (1962) *The Modern Theology of Tradition*, London: Darton Longman & Todd

McPherson, T. (1967) *Political Obligation*, London: Routledge & Kegan Paul; New York: Humanities Press

Madge, J. (1962) *The Origins of Scientific Sociology*, New

York: Free Press

Marcuse, H. (1972) 'A Study on Authority', in *Studies in Critical Philosophy,* London: NLB

Maritain, J. (1940) 'Democracy and Authority', in *Scholaticism and Politics,* New York: Macmillan

Marshall, T.H. (1937) 'Authority and the Family', *Sociological Review,* 29

Marsilius of Padua (1951) *Defensor Pacis,* New York: Columbia UP

Martin, R. (1974) 'Wolff's defence of philosophical anarchism', *Philosophical Review,* 24

—— (1977) *The Sociology of Power,* London: Routledge & Kegan Paul

Martineau, J. (1905) *The Seat of Authority in Religion,* 5th edn., London: Lindsey

Mead, M. (1951) *Soviet Attitudes Toward Authority: an interdisciplinary approach to problems of Soviet character,* New York: McGraw Hill

Merriam, C.E. (1934) *Political Power: its composition and incidence,* New York: McGraw Hill

Milgram, S. (1974) *Obedience to Authority,* London: Tavistock; New York: Harper & Row

Mill, J.S. (1960) *On Liberty,* London: OUP

Miller, W.B. (1955) 'Two Concepts of Authority', *American Anthropologist,* 57

Molnar, T. (1976) *Authority and its Enemies,* New York: Arlington House

Mommsen, Theodor (1952) *Römisches Staatsrecht III,* Basel: Schwabe

Murphy, A.E. (1952) 'An Ambiguity in Professor Simon's Philosophy of Democratic Government', *Philosophical Review,* 59

Murray, R.H. (1929) 'Conscience and Authority', *Contemporary Review,* 135

Newman, J.H. (1955) *An Essay in Aid of a Grammar of Assent,* Garden City, NY: Image

Nisbet, R. (1972) 'The Nemesis of Authority', *Encounter,* 39. Also in *Intercollegiate Review,* 8

—— (1976) *Twilight of Authority,* London: Heinemann

Nomos I: Authority (1958) Friedrich, C.J. (ed.), Cambridge, Mass: Harvard UP

Nomos XIX, Anarchism (1978) Pennock, J.R. and Chapman, R.W. (eds.), New York: NYU Press

Orr, R.R. (1967) *Reason and Authority: The Thought of William Chillingworth,* London: OUP

Otten, C.M. (1970) *University Authority and the Student: The Berkeley Experience,* Berkeley: University of California Press

Parekh, B. (ed.) (1973) *Bentham's Political Thought,* London: Croom Helm

Patten, S. (1977) 'Milgram's shocking experiments', *Philosophy,* 52

Peabody, R.L. (1961) 'Perceptions of Organisational Authority: A Comparative Analysis', *Administrative Science Quarterly,* 6

Perkins, L.H. (1972) 'On Reconciling Autonomy and Authority', *Ethics,* 82

Peters, R.S. (1965) *Authority, Responsibility and Education,* New York: Atherton

—— (1966) *Ethics and Education,* London: Allen & Unwin

Petrick, M.J. (1968) 'Supreme Court and Authority Acceptance', *Western Political Quarterly,* 21

Pitkin, Hannah (1966) 'Obligation and Consent', *American Political Science Review,* 60

Polanyi, M. (1946) 'Authority and Conscience', in *Science, Faith and Society,* London: OUP

Porn, Ingmar (1970) *The Logic of Power,* Oxford: Blackwell

Pranger, R.J. (1966) 'An Explanation for Why Final Political Authority is Necessary', *American Political Science Review,* 60

Pye, L.W. (1968) *The Spirit of Chinese Politics: A Psychocultural Study of the Authority Crisis in Political Development,* Cambridge, Mass: MIT Press

Quinton, A. (ed.) (1967) *Political Philosophy,* London: OUP

Rahman, Fazlur (1966) *Islam,* London: Weidenfeld & Nicolson

Rapaport, E. (1976) 'Anarchism and authority in Marx's socialist politics', *European Journal of Sociology,* 2

Raphael, D.D. (1970) 'Sovereignty, Power and Authority' and 'Liberty and Authority', in *Problems of Political Philosophy,* New York: Praeger

Ray, J.J. (1976) 'Do authoritarians hold authoritarian attitudes?' *Human Relations,* 29

Rokeach, M. (1960) *The Open and Closed Mind: Investigations into the Nature of Belief Systems and Personality Systems,* New York: Basic Books

Roth, L. (1959) 'Authority, Religion and Law', *Hibbert Journal,* 58

Russell, B.A. (1949) *Authority and the Individual,* New York: Simon and Schuster

Santayana, G. (1951) 'Rational authority' and 'Rival Seats of Authority', in *Dominations and Powers,* New York: Scribners

Schaar, J.H. (1961) *Escape from Authority: The Perspectives of Erich Fromm,* New York: Basic Books

Schiller, M. (1972) 'Political Authority, Self-Defence, and Pre-Emptive War', *Canadian Journal of Philosophy,* I

Schneewind, J.B. (ed.) (1969) *Mill,* London: Macmillan

Schneider, H.W. (1952) 'Santayana and Realistic Conceptions of Authority', *Journal of Philosophy,* 49

Scott, W.R. *et al.* (1967) 'Organisational Evaluation and Authority', *Administrative Science Quarterly,* 12

Sennett, Richard (1980) *Authority,* New York: Knopf

Shklar, J.N. (1964) 'Rousseau's Images of Authority', *American Political Science Review,* 58

Shuster, G.N. (ed.) (1967) *Freedom and Authority in the West,* Notre Dame: Notre Dame UP

Siegel, S. (1954) 'Certain Determinants and Correlates of Authoritarianism', *Genetic Psychology Monographs,* 49

Silberman, L.H. (1962) 'Paradoxes of Freedom and Authority', *Hibbert Journal,* 60

Simon, H.A. (1957) 'Authority', in Conrad Arensberg *et al.* (eds.), *Research in Industrial Relations,* New York: Harper

Simon, Y. (1950) *Nature and Functions of Authority,* Milwaukee: Marquette University Press

Sinyavsky, Andrei (1960) *The Trial Begins,* London: Collins

Skinner, Quentin (1978) *Foundations of Modern Political Thought,* Cambridge: CUP

Southern, R.W. (1962) *The Making of the Middle Ages,* London: Hutchinson

Southgate, W.M. (1962) *John Jewel and the Problem of Doctinal Authority,* Cambridge, Mass: Harvard University Press

Spencer, M.E. (1970) 'Weber on Legitimate Norms and

Authority', *British Journal of Sociology,* 21

Spitz, D. (1949) *Patterns of Anti-democratic Thought,* New York: Macmillan

Stahl, O.G. (1958) 'The Network of Authority', *Public Administration Review,* 18

—— (1960) 'More on the Network of Authority', *Public Administration Review,* 20

Starobinski, J. (1977) 'Criticism and authority', *Daedalus,* 106

Stirner, M. (1971) *The Ego and His Own: The Case of the Individual Against Authority,* trans. S.T. Byington, New York: Harper

Strickland, D.A. (1970) 'Authority as a Reference Problem', *Ethics,* 80

Tavard, G.A. (1959) *Holy Writ or Holy Church,* London: Sheed and Ward

Thomas, S.B. (1969) 'Authority and the Law in the United States, 1968', *Ethics,* 79

Todd, J.M. (ed.) (1962) *Problems of Authority,* Baltimore: Helicon

Tritton, A.S. (1951) *Islam: Beliefs and Practices,* London: Hutchinson

Tucker, R.C. (1968) 'The Theory of Charismatic Leadership', *Daedalus,* 97

Tussman, Joseph (1960) *Obligation and the Body Politic,* New York: Oxford University Press

Ullmann, W. (1961) *Principles of Government and Politics in the Middle Ages,* London: Methuen

Van Fleet, D. (1973) 'The Need-hierarchy and theories of authority', *Human Relations,* 26

Walsh, W.H. (1971) 'Knowledge in Its Social Setting', *Mind,* 80

Weber, Max (1946) *From Max Weber: Essays on Sociology,* trans. H.H. Gerth and C. Wright Mills, New York: OUP

—— (1947) *Theory of Social and Economic Organization,* trans. by A.M. Henderson and T. Parsons, London: Hodge

—— (1961) 'The Types of Authority', in *Theories of Society,* New York: Free Press

—— (1968) *Max Weber on Charisma and Institution Building: Selected Papers,* S.N. Eisenstadt (ed.) Chicago: University of Chicago Press

Weil, Simone (1949) *L'Enracinement,* Paris: Gallimard

—— (1958) *Oppression and Liberty,* trans. from the French

by A. Wills and J. Petrie, London: Routledge

Weldon, T.D. (1953) *The Vocabulary of Politics,* Baltimore: Penguin

Westby, D.L. (1966) 'Typology of Authority in Complex Organisations', *Social Forces,* 44

White, J., Alter, R. and Rardin, M. (1965) 'Authoritarianism, Dogmatism and Usage of Conceptual Categories', *Journal of Personality and Social Psychology,* 2

Whyte, William (1957) *The Organization Man,* London: Cape

Willhoite, F. (1976) 'Primates and political authority', *American Political Science Review,* 70

Wilson, F.G. (1937) 'The Prelude to Authority', *American Political Science Review,* 31

Wilson, J.A. *et al.* (1954) *Authority and Law in the Ancient Orient,* Baltimore: American Oriental Society

Wirszubski, Chaim (1960) *Libertas as a Political Ideal at Rome during the Late Republic and Early Principate,* Cambridge: CUP

Wolff, R.P. (ed.) (1966) *Political Man and Social Man: readings in political philosophy,* New York: Random House

—— (1970) *In Defense of Anarchism,* New York: Harper & Row

Wolpert, J.F. (1965) 'Toward a Sociology of Authority', in A.W. Gouldner (ed.), *Studies in Leadership,* New York: Russell

Yelaja, S.A. (ed.) (1911) *Authority and Social Work: Concept and Use,* Toronto: University of Toronto Press

Young, G. (1974) 'Authority', *Canadian Journal of Philosophy,* 3